Dr. Mike Jaffe has shared his compelling life story that you will want to read. Journey with him from his roots as the child of nominal Jewish parents, but devout Jewish grandparents, all the way to his present ministry as chair of the church ministries department at Evangel University. He tasted the life of rebellion, drugs, and the famous Woodstock festival until, in the midst of emptiness, he was witnessed to by Jesus freaks and his life took a dramatic turn. Dr. Jaffe's account is more than his life story—it's a representative story of the transformation Christ brings to lives that are broken and lost. Your life will be enriched for reading this absorbing autobiography.

George O. Wood
General Superintendent
General Council of the Assemblies of God (U.S.A.)

Found is the poignant story of a young man growing up in the upheaval of the 1960s. Michael Jaffe's journey of personal tragedy is told through thr iconic fabric of the '60s including LSD, Woodstock, and the Jesus freaks. More than the tale of an aging Boomer, Jaffe's story is increasingly the norm in contemporary America. The dissolving of family life in our nation impacts young people who are set adrift to find themselves in increasingly self-destructive activity.

Michael Jaffe's retelling of his life story is laced with personal reflection that has offered a legacy to his own sons. At the same time it is a gift to those 'riders in the storms" of twenty-first century making. *Found* is not only a testimony to the grace of God, but it is a statement of faith bound up in human fabric. *Found* is not just a book title—it is a statement of eternal truth. This book tells a wonderful story, but offers a mature and clear explanation of the value and purpose of every person's life from a seasoned pastor and teacher.

Michael Jaffe's life story is more than a good read, it is evidence that a transforming encounter with Jesus Christ is a clear affirmation that the gospel "abundantly pardons and saves to the uttermost. "

Byron D. Klaus
Former President, Assemblies of God Theological Seminary (1999–2015)
Springfield, Missouri

Michael Jaffe's *Found* traces the arc of his life. It is an engaging story of promise, loss, and promise regained. I grew up in the same part of New Jersey in the same era, so the unfolding story resonates deeply. He shares the story of his life with an authenticity that makes this a compelling read. Even if you didn't grow up in south Jersey in the 1950s and 1960s, you will be drawn into his story. In Jaffe's writing I am reminded of the words of author Gail Caldwell:

> "I know now that we never get over great losses; we absorb them, and they carve us into different, often kinder, creatures. . . . We tell the story to get them back, to capture the traces of footfalls through the snow."

Through great loss Michael Jaffe was "carved into a different creature" by power of the gospel and he shares profound truths in a simple straightforward way in this memoir.

Alan MacDonald
Pastor, Global Engagement Fairfax Community Church
Fairfax, Virginia

Found is a compelling account of God's amazing grace in the life of Mike Jaffe—from a grieving young Jewish lad, to a rebellious teen caught up in the Woodstock and drug culture of late 1960s and 1970s, to a Jesus freak who found Christ, to a pastor and husband and father, to a theology professor and grandfather. This is a moving story of God's faithfulness and grace and redemption.

The subtitle "A Story of One Life Transformation" is misleading. When you read this personal reflection, you will find that the transformation of grace received extends far beyond a single life story. It includes family members and friends and a new generation of young men and women who are touched by the life of this professor who can sing with John Newton "I once was lost but now am found. Amazing grace, how sweet the sound."

Carol Taylor
President, Evangel University
Springfield, Missouri

From Judaism to the drug culture to a transformed life, Michael Jaffe recounts his life journey in a remarkably candid and inspiring way. *Found* drew me in and left me in awe of the wonderful grace of God. I am so grateful for Michael's transparent storytelling as well as his continued influence in the lives of thousands of young people preparing for ministry.

James Bradford
General Secretary
General Council of the Assemblies of God (U.S.A.)

Found

A Story of One Life Transformation

Michael Jaffe

Cover design by www.JesseAdamWilson.com

Published by Makarios Publishing, Springfield, MO, USA
www.MakariosPublishing.com

ISBN: 978-0-9969809-0-6

Printed in United States of America

Contents

Foreword

The decision to write *Found* was made after conversations with all three of my sons—Josh, Ben, and Nate. These conversations took place on three distinct occasions, taking place over six years. They were all young adults at the time. In separate situations, I told my life story to my sons, a story each had never heard. The reason I waited so long was rooted in the complexity of my emotional inability to fully deal with certain elements of my past.

My first conversation was with Ben, my second born, when he was twenty-two years old. The two of us planned a trip together to New Jersey and New York. Our plan was to visit my sister Alice and her son Nicholas, as well as old friends from Middletown and Cazenovia, New York. During the trip, the subject of my life prior to my knowing Jesus came up. I shared about my life from the beginning and I was amazed at Ben's interest. He was deeply impacted.

When we arrived in my hometown of Vineland, New Jersey, the two of us took a tour. I showed Ben the house in which I had grown up, the Sons of Jacob synagogue in which I had received my bar mitzvah, and the street where my grandparents had lived. Unfortunately, their house had been torn town. This part of the trip was extremely interesting to Ben and therapeutic in many ways for me.

Sometime after returning home from our trip, I recounted the experience with my wife, Barb. She strongly felt I should have similar conversations with our other two sons. Still feeling less than comfortable sharing my story, I waited for the right opportunities.

The next opportunity came four years later when I shared my story with Nate who was then twenty years old. On this occasion the circumstances were very different. As I recall, we were having a disagreement relating to parental authority. Out of nowhere, I began sharing how my early life lacked the important component of a fatherly influence, which in turn led to my story. Again, the impact on Nate was clearly evident.

Finally, one evening about two years after my conversation with Nate, the Lord provided an opportunity to briefly tell aspects of my early life to Josh (then thirty-one) and his wife, Brooke. Aspects of the story clearly drew an emotional response. Josh told me that he wanted to hear much more.

As time passed, I began entertaining the thought of putting my story down on paper as a record of the beginnings of how the knowledge of Jesus came to the Jaffe family. The more I thought about it, the more I felt it important to write down the story for posterity. After all, to my knowledge no Jaffe from my ancestry has ever professed a faith in Christ. If my story is where faith in Jesus begins as it relates to our family, there should be a record of it. Secondly, the mere existence of my sons and grandchildren is wholly linked to this story.

Finally, in the spring 2014 semester, I sat in on Dr. Marty Middlestadt's Pentecost class taught at Evangel University where I currently hold the positions of professor of Preaching and Leadership and Church Ministries Department chair. One segment of the class emphasized the role and power of story in the communication of the gospel. Each student was encouraged to engage his or her own story. As I thought about my own, I became convinced of the need to engage with my personal narrative.

The months that followed have been enriching and satisfying. During these months, I have experienced the wonders of His grace afresh and anew. There is real power and strength that comes with contemplating the work of God in one's life. I agree wholeheartedly with the sentiments of the songwriter who wrote:

Great is Thy faithfulness, Oh God my Father;
There is no shadow of turning with Thee;
Thou changest not, thy compassions, they fail not;
As Thou hast been, Thou forever will be.

Pardon for sin and a peace that endureth
Thine own dear presence to cheer and to guide;
Strength for today and bright hope for tomorrow,
Blessings all mine, with ten thousand beside!

Great is Thy faithfulness!
Great is Thy faithfulness!
Morning by morning new mercies I see.
All I have needed Thy hand hath provided;
Great is Thy faithfulness, Lord unto me!

"Great Is Thy Faithfulness"
Words by Thomas O. Chisholm

Part 1:

What It Means to Be Lost

Part 1

Introduction to Part 1

Amazing grace how sweet the sound
That saved a wretch like me.
I once was lost *but now am found*
Was blind but now I see.
—John Newton

"For the Son of Man came to seek and to save the lost"
—Luke 19:10

"As for you, you were dead in your transgressions and sins, in which you used to live when you followed the ways of this world and of the ruler of the kingdom of the air, the spirit who is now at work in those who are disobedient. All of us also lived among them at one time."
—Ephesians 2:1–3

As King Theoden sat slumped upon his throne, so much had changed. His kingdom had come apart and he had been reduced to a figurehead monarch. Theoden had fallen under the evil influence of the wicked wizard Saruman. Those who loved Theoden stood by helplessly as their once-great king and the kingdom he led deteriorated before their very eyes. A seemingly invincible army bent on destroying all the inhabitants of the kingdom of Rohan was massing to accomplish its total destruction. No defensive strategies were being implemented. The people looked to their king, but he had become completely unresponsive. Theoden had become a bewildered, devastated, and hopelessly lost ruler.

Lovers of *The Lord of the Rings* trilogy will recognize this scene from *The Two Towers,* the middle book of J. R. R. Tolkien's masterpiece. It is an emotional heart-wrenching episode that represented the point where the king hit rock bottom. Something had to change and change immediately or all would be lost for both the king and the entire realm of Rohan that his ancestors had long led so nobly.

King Theoden's desperate circumstances remind me of people in life. There are times when people come to the point of crisis. They hit the proverbial rock bottom where they find themselves similarly bewildered and crushed. Such circumstances can be the natural result of humanity's fallen state. There comes a time when all can seem hopeless.

Among the many expressions the New Testament uses to describe the human condition apart from Christ is the term *lost*. The word *lost* implies a number of things. It connotes a sense of separation. In the biblical sense as it relates to the human race, it describes a state of being separated and alienated from the Creator. Humans are lost and completely unable to find their way back to the One who gave them life in the first place.

The Bible makes clear that sin leaves men and women dead and utterly nonresponsive when it comes to God's intent and purpose for their lives. This means they are unable to think as God thinks and act as God acts. People end up seeking their own solutions while at the same time finding themselves feeling more and more confused. At the heart of sin is selfishness, a selfishness that often leads them to do whatever is necessary to overcome this deep sense of alienation.

Their relationships with others result in even greater life predicaments. People live in a world that is populated with others who are attempting and failing to weave their way through the same struggles. Fallen human beings take a toll on each other, leaving one another worse off. One generation leaves the consequences of its lostness to the next and its posterity to inherit its abundant sufferings and struggles.

The more you study the Bible the more you recognize that it presents sin from a number of different perspectives.

- Sin is viewed from the lens of an internal disposition inclining people to do things that are wrong. In other words, we are not sinners because we sin; rather we sin because we are sinners.
- Sin is considered to be a state of rebelliousness and disobedience. People instinctively know what is required of them. but choose to do otherwise.
- Sin is understood to be something that disables and distorts our character. People become futile in their thinking and actions.
- Sin is seen as a failure to meet God's standards. Our motives and actions fall short of the requirements of a morally pure Creator. Lastly,
- Sin is revealed to be a challenge to God's rightful authority over His creation. It places human beings in control over all decision making.[1]

The truth is we are all in the same boat, trying to navigate our way through life's stormy seas. Although we may outwardly appear to be doing fine, these outward appearances are deceiving to ourselves and others. For some the deception works. They are able to convince the world around them that all is well. For others however, their state of being lost is obvious. Their lives are self-destructive and devastating to others.

Being lost, of course, also implies being in a state of confusion and disorientation. There is immense pain that results. Our relationships with others go bad. Our hearts are empty. Our lives are lived without meaning. For many, a sense of hopelessness sets in.

It is in this context that I wish to tell the first part of my story. In many respects, it is no different from other stories. True, it will contain a set of events that are different from many who have gone through similar journeys. But it left me in the same state that has characterized countless millions of others. I was in every sense of the word—*lost.*

[1]Millard Erickson, *Introducing Christian Doctrine,* (Grand Rapids: Baker Academic, 2001).

Chapter 1

My Early Years

"The Spirit of the Sovereign Lord is on me, because the Lord has anointed me to preach good news to the poor. He has sent me to bind up the brokenhearted, to proclaim freedom for the captives and release from darkness for the prisoners, to proclaim the year of the Lord's favor and the day of vengeance of our God, to comfort all who mourn, and provide for those who grieve in Zion–to bestow on them a crown of beauty instead of ashes, the oil of joy instead of mourning, and a garment of praise instead of a spirit of despair. They will be called oaks of righteousness, a planting of the Lord for the display of his splendor."

—Isaiah 61:1–3

A numb ache" is the only way I can attempt to describe it. The truth is no words can adequately portray the feelings of a thirteen-year-old when a vital foundation of life is taken away. There was a sense of finality. And there was an equal sense of emptiness. It was a devastating feeling of loss accompanied by complete confusion.

The four weeks that preceded the fateful Saturday were full of apprehension and dread. My sister Alice and I went to school and kept a relatively normal schedule. My sister was in her first year of high school while I had just transitioned to junior high. Beneath the normalcy of adolescence, both of us along with Mom were becoming increasingly fearful. With each passing day our hope was receding and a sense of dread was growing within us.

Every evening at about six o'clock, I would take my place on the sofa as was typical for me and wait for Dad to come home. Somehow I felt that if I could recreate the usual circumstances of his arrival, he would pull up in the driveway as he always had. But each day, I was disappointed. Each night I would go to bed with the hope that the next evening would be different. I'm sure Mom and Alice were doing similar things. Hope is a necessary ingredient in life. It keeps us going.

All our hopes were dashed that Saturday afternoon in early April when a city policeman arrived at the door. I was in the kitchen. Mom and Alice were in the living room. I remember the look on his face. It was solemn and expressionless. As he walked in the door, he said he had news. In my heart at that moment, I instinctively knew what he was going to say. What I did not know however was that this day would be one that would set my life on a journey that I could never in my wildest imaginings have foreseen.

A Salvation History

Each person's life is a story. It is complete with all the elements that make for a story. There are characters, big events, seemingly irrelevant detail, pivotal moments: and a climax. While the story is unfolding, it is impossible to know the importance of the elements; but in time, many of these become clear. Because a person is living the story, that person cannot know precisely how it will end.

For the Christian however there are significant differences. The first is the knowledge that the personal story is part of a greater grand narrative, God's story. The Christian should know that although he or she cannot know the precise ending, it is part of that grand narrative, one that is written by a loving God. With this in mind, I commence the telling of my own personal story. I do so recognizing that it is part of a greater whole. My story represents my salvation history which is only a small part of the salvation history that has been going on since the beginning of humankind.

My Beginnings

It is very important for believers to apprehend and appreciate the truth that God is always at work in their lives. This applies to life both before and after conversion. He is at every one of life's street corners, always present and always involved. Some of His acts in our lives are exceedingly painful while others are full of incredible joy, but He is present in all things. As I begin my story, I hope the reader will find the ability to practice one of the most important elements in spiritual growth—choosing to express gratitude for everything life brings. Believers can do this because God has a purpose in all of life's experiences.

My story begins in the city of Vineland, New Jersey. Vineland is a city with a population of approximately sixty thousand, located in south New Jersey about halfway between Philadelphia and Atlantic City. It is named for its many grapevines and in some way was associated with Thomas Bramwell Welch who founded Welch's Grape Juice. Southern New Jersey is known for its great sandy soil that can grow a tremendous variety of crops. For this reason New Jersey is called "the Garden State." While much of New Jersey is heavily populated, south Jersey is primarily agricultural, with large vegetable truck farms.

My first memory was standing in the street, watching builders build the home that my family would soon occupy. I was three years old and the anticipation of a new house must have been exciting. Why else would the event be my first recollection of life? The house at 712 Third Street Terrace would be a simple, small, ranch-style home with three bedrooms, one bath, a living room, and an eat-in kitchen. It had greenish-gray shingles on the exterior. Clearly it was nothing much to look at, but it would be my home throughout my childhood and a place to frequent from time to time during what would become my tumultuous adolescence.

I can easily remember most of the families who lived throughout the neighborhood. The Feldmans lived on one side of us and the Behrigs on the other side and across the street (two brothers and their families.) Next to the Feldmans lived the Lamberts, followed by another family that escapes my memory and then the Duffys. Behind our house was Third Street. There lived the Boormans, some other family I can't place, the Deans, the Bloughs, and the Spencers. I can remember that Debbie Boorman had a crush on me (or so I thought at the time) and I had a crush on Dee Dee Blough.

I was born to Hyman and Pearl (Broidy) Jaffe on a cold winter's day in 1952. Alice, my only sibling, preceded me into this world just over two years earlier. My mother's side of the family was of Eastern European origin, of what is called the Ashkenazim strain of Judaism. My father, who was born in Leeds, England, was from the Sephardic line that migrated through the Mediterranean to Spain and western Europe. Although both families were Jewish, their levels of observance were as different as night and day. My mother's family was deeply orthodox, while my father's was nominal.

Mom was born in Easton, Pennsylvania, in 1913. Her parents had immigrated to the United States from eastern Europe around the turn of the century. Like many European immigrants of that time, Mom followed the determined and sometimes overbearing (by modern standards) dictates of her parents. She quit school after the ninth grade because she was needed at home. Mom had two brothers, Leo her fraternal twin and Eli who was three years younger. Mom and Uncle Leo were timid and easily overpowered by those with stronger wills. Eli, on the other hand, was assertive and much more successful in life. All three siblings married very late. In fact, only Mom married early enough to have children. She married Dad when she was thirty-six. Oddly and fortunately for Alice and me, Dad moved into the triplex my grandparents rented out and met Mom. They soon married, just in the nick of time for her to give birth to a couple of children.

Contemplating how my parents met leaves me in awe of both the sovereignty of God and the impact of the smallest choices we make in life. As a result of Dad's decision to move into my grandparents' triplex, my sister and I are alive. My three sons and five grandchildren whom I will introduce later also owe their existence to (among other things, of course) this seemingly insignificant life decision. All their children who follow in succeeding generations will in some way owe their existence to this event. How wonderful and awesome are God's ways!

Dad's story was markedly different from Mom's. For reasons I will elaborate on later, much of his life has always been a mystery to me. Here is what I do know. My father was born in Leeds, England in 1909. He emigrated to the United States when he was ten along with his older brother Herman and younger sister Mildred. Not long after arriving in the United States, my dad's father left his wife and shortly afterward she died. Dad and his younger sister were placed in an orphanage, somewhere in Georgia. Because Herman was old enough to work, he escaped Dad's fate. Apparently, however he was able to make enough money to help Dad and my aunt Mildred leave the orphanage. From what I later learned, Dad took responsibility for his younger sister and took care of her for a number of years. Undoubtedly, his life was a hard one, a fact that would deeply impact Alice and me much later.

Rose Peritzman, my maternal grandmother, was married to a man who died prior to my birth. She later married a man named Isaac Salter, the only grandfather I ever really knew. My stepgrandfather was a deeply influential figure in my early years. Grand Pop Salter, as we knew him, was a kind, deeply Orthodox Jew who loved our family. He raised me to be an observant Jewish boy, encouraging me to take the role of religious head of the family. This role included the observance of all Old Testament feast days described in the Book of Leviticus. He always made sure that I understood their meaning. Grand Pop Salter also paid for me to attend Hebrew School, where I would learn to read Hebrew in preparation for my Bar Mitzvah when I became thirteen years of age.

Grandma Rose was what might be called a typical woman from the old country. Outside of the religious matters that were Grand Pop Salter's domain, she "ran" the family to the degree Dad allowed her. I should add, however, that I never detected any animosity between her and my father. Her will was strong and clearly overpowered Mom. But like Grand Pop Salter, she dearly loved her children and grandchildren.

For Orthodox Jews, Saturdays constitute a Sabbath unto the Lord. Actually the Sabbath begins at sundown on Friday and extends to sundown on Saturday. Jews consider each day to begin in the evening according to the words of Genesis "And there was evening, and there was morning—the first day" (Genesis 1:5, see also vss. 8, 13, 19, 23, 31). Grand Pop Salter was a respected man in the local Orthodox synagogue. Every Sabbath in his later years, he would get a ride with a man to *shul* which is Yiddish for "synagogue." They would park their car around the block and walk to the synagogue. Grand Pop Salter had a bad heart and although he used to walk to *shul* when he was younger, he was unable to after he turned seventy. Apart from this one indiscretion out of necessity, he unwaveringly observed the Sabbath.

Because of the commitment of my grandparents to the Jewish Sabbath, Sundays were generally the time for family gatherings for the Jaffes and Salters. Sundays were routinely spent at the home of Grandma and Grand Pop Salter. I remember regularly going with my dad to the corner store to purchase two quart bottles of soda and a newspaper. Dad, although he had only completed the seventh grade, was an avid reader especially when it came to politics, sports and current events. Typical Sundays consisted of dinner cooked by Grandma Salter (typical eastern-European Jewish dishes) and hopefully for Dad and me, the opportunity to watch our beloved Phillies lose another baseball game. They were invariably a terrible team during my childhood years.

As for other members of the family, most of my recollections involve family on my mother's side. My favorite uncle was my extremely meek Uncle Leo who had a wonderful sense of humor. He clearly needed it to survive the dominant females in his life. His wife, my Aunt Rae, bossed him around and ridiculed his meek spirit regularly although in a warm sort of way. It was clear they loved each other even though she wore the pants in the relationship, without question. When not under the dominion of my aunt, my Grandmother Rose was waiting to tell her son what to do and when to do it. In response, he would only laugh and quietly make some sly remark to my sister and me, always out of earshot of any of the dominating women of his life.

Poor but Not Unhappy

Thinking back to my childhood years, there were few unhappy memories. My sister Alice and I were reasonably secure in these early years. There was very little money but our family managed to scrape by. We would find out later however that the family financial situation was more ominous than we understood as children.

Most of my early memories revolve around my father. I can remember waiting on the couch for him to get home from work. He worked for Uncle Herman who owned Jaffe's Auto Parts at the corner of Third and Wood Streets in Vineland. My father was merely an employee of my uncle and was paid eighty dollars a week, low to average income even by the standards of the 1960s. Each day I would take my place on the living room sofa and wait for his arrival. He would generally bring something home like a bag of cookies. It wasn't much, but it was something memorable for me.

Dad had a love for sports. I recollect playing catch with him in the front yard. I recall him teaching me how to hit a baseball and catch a football. My most significant memories with Dad have to do with the two of us listening to the Phillies play on the radio. We had no TV and there were times when we didn't even have a radio except the ones in our 1950 and later 1954 Plymouths. Summer evenings we would put the car battery on auxiliary and listen to the games. I clearly remember burning "punks" to keep the mosquitos at bay. I would often plead with Dad to allow me to listen to "one more inning," a request he would more times than not deny, at least when school was still in session. Of course, he had to wake up early for work as well, so we seldom actually listened to a game all the way through.

Occasionally my dad, sister, and I could go to a game at historic Connie Mack Stadium, located at Twenty-first and Lehigh in north Philly. I always tried to persuade Dad to get tickets to a doubleheader which in the 1960s consisted of two games for the price of one. Typically the doubleheaders took place on Sunday afternoons, enabling us to get home at a reasonable time. Dad would get discount coupons for reserved seats ($ 2.25) at the ballpark if he purchased a minimal amount of groceries at the local ACME market. To my way of thinking, nothing was more fun than a day at the ballpark even though the Phillies were generally a losing team during my childhood.

Other memories included trips to Riverview Amusement Park in south Jersey. Mom never accompanied us for reasons I never really understood at the time. Dad would purchase a three-dollar book of ride tickets for Alice and me, and that would have to last the entire day. To make the ride tickets last the day, he would occupy us with other things at the park like feeding bread crumbs to the large catfish which were stocked in a relatively large pool. We understood Dad's budget and were content with what he could afford. On occasion, he would buy an additional one-dollar book of tickets if he could manage it and that was an unexpected treat.

Salt and Pepper

Physically, I had one distinguishing characteristic that separated me from any other child I knew. At the age of nine, my hair began turning gray. My hair did not turn gray in the normal way from the roots up. It was a pigmentation problem inherited from my mother's side. Hair strands would start out black and begin turning gray as they grew. This distinguishing physical feature would accompany me throughout childhood, adolescence, and beyond.

My first traumatic experience came in the fourth grade. It was the first day of school and the teacher was calling the roll for the first time. He got to my name and looked up to see who the student was that corresponded to the name. I purposely sat near the back to avoid notice. He stared before exclaiming, "My word, you have gray hair!" He then proceeded to the back of the classroom to determine if his eyes were playing tricks on him. Needless to say the entire class laughed. I didn't know whether to laugh too or sit there embarrassed. I think I did both.

My premature gray hair would garner attention wherever I went during my formative years. Sometimes people would simply stare. On other occasions, I would hear a person in the background exclaim, "Look at that boy! He has gray hair!" The most embarrassing by far were the times little old ladies would stop me and ask, "Is it real?" It became a real conversation piece for people wherever I went. This biological oddity would later become significant in a way I could not have foreseen.

Three Dollars a Week

I distinctly remember one early summer weekend afternoon at supper when Dad announced that he had persuaded Uncle Herman to hire me to deliver parts on my bicycle to the nearby auto repair shops. Dad was alone in the store and often found himself having to close the store for brief periods in order to deliver parts to these shops. Hiring me would be cheaper than hiring a full-time delivery man. Dad stated he was holding out for "a dollar a day" but Uncle Herman was not willing to pay more than three dollars a week. The difference between three dollars and six did not matter to me in the least. I had just secured, with the help of my father, my first real job. I was eleven years old at the time and having a job in the summer was exciting to me, especially since I would be working with Dad.

Days at Jaffe's Auto Parts were fun during the summer of

1963. I would ride my bike there arriving sometime mid-morning and deliver parts when needed, but a lot of time was spent watching Dad wait on customers. Occasionally I would persuade him to give me a free six-and-a-half-ounce Coca Cola or seven-ounce Sprite from the soda machine. These were the versions in the now antique glass bottles. For some reason, sodas in the glass bottles tasted so much better than the plastic bottle versions that came later. When things were especially slow, Dad and I would sit in the back and listen to the Phillies games on the radio if they were playing during the afternoon. The Phillies broadcaster was a man by the name of Byrum (By) Saam. He broadcasted Phillies games for many years along with fellow broadcasters Bill Campbell and former Phillies great Richie Ashburn. These voices were staples in my youth.

1963 was a year that was better than most for longsuffering Phillies fans. It was a winning season, a season that would lead to a better, but extraordinarily painful, season in 1964. For my part, 1963 represented the good times of growing up. It was a year of bonding with Dad. It is a current reminder that there were good times in my childhood. I think everyone needs to have pleasant memories to look back on when things turn bad in their lives. Suffice it to say that the summer of '63 was that time. It was a year that would turn out to be my last carefree time as a child.

Chapter 2
The Sons of Jacob

"These commandments that I give you today are to be on your hearts. Impress them on your children. Talk about them when you sit at home and when you walk along the road, when you lie down and when you get up. Tie them as symbols on your hands and bind them on your foreheads. Write them on the doorframes of your houses and on your gates."
—Deuteronomy 6:6–9

I marvel at the resilience of the Jewish people. Their best characteristic is their desire to remember. No other people has such an obsession with memory.
—Elie Wiesel

Tevye [spoken to God]: I know, I know. We are Your chosen people. But once in a while, can't You choose someone else?
—Fiddler on the Roof

Many of us are familiar with this well-known line in the musical *Fiddler on the Roof.* It highlights the plight of the Jewish people for centuries. Suffering, persecution, death, and other forms of hardship have characterized their history.

What does it mean to be a Jew? The answer to this question

partially explains the ability of the Jewish people to endure. Is "Jewish" a religion, a nationality, or both? The answer is both! It is the sum of an ancient relationship between a people and their God. It is also an unbroken chain of ancestry that has endured for nearly 3,500 years.

My Grandparents' Influence

An extremely important part of my story is my formative years in Judaism. There are a number of facets to this, but I will only allude to the most significant elements, those steeped within my memory. In many ways my early in experience in Judaism, specifically the years spent at an Orthodox synagogue in my hometown of Vineland, New Jersey, would in an odd way help draw my life to Jesus.

The synagogue was a relatively small congregation called "The Sons of Jacob." It was located on Grape Street between Third and Fourth Streets and was also known by the members of the congregation as "The Grape Street *shul*." My grandfather Salter was a respected elder there, and as I stated earlier, an important influence in my life when I was a child.

Grand Pop Salter, as my sister and I called him, was by far the strongest religious influence in our family. Dad was absent when it came to practicing Judaism. He was a nominal Jew in every sense. All religious activity took place on my mother's side of the family, most notably under my grandfather's tutelage. What is at least a little odd is that he was actually my stepgrandfather.

I have many memories of celebrating the regular Jewish festivals. There are five major festivals that are deeply religious in nature. They are *Rosh Hashanah* (the Jewish New Year), *Yom Kippur* (the Day of Atonement), *Succot* (the Feast of Tabernacles or the Feast of Booths), *Pesach* (the Passover), and *Shavou'ot* (the Feast of Pentecost). These are listed in order from the perspective of the secular Jewish calendar, not in order of importance. The *Shabbat* or Sabbath is also sacred in Orthodox Judaism. Grand Pop Salter would take me with him to *shul* as I got older and I would watch him *daven* (Jewish ritual prayer). While I have memories of celebrating all of the holy days, my most significant recollections revolve around the celebration of *Pesach* or the Passover.

The Passover festival is actually celebrated over eight days, which encompasses the entire Feast of the Unleavened Bread, but the first evening of the festival that ushers in the celebration is the focal point. The Passover Seder was a big event in the Salter house. Grandma Salter would prepare for it by meticulously "cleaning out the leaven from her home." In Orthodox Jewish homes, virtually everything in the kitchen that was commonly used during the year had to be boxed up and put aside. A completely new set of utensils, dishes, and almost everything else imaginable to serve food had to be brought out for use during the eight-day holiday. All foods in the pantry and refrigerator had to be removed and set aside in similar fashion. Only foods that were kosher for Passover were allowed to be eaten. In other words, foods that were ordinarily kosher for the rest of the year were not allowed during this period of celebration and observance.

Grand Pop Salter took a great deal of time teaching me both the importance of the annual festivals and how a dedicated Jew must observe them. During the Passover, this included the elements of the Seder among other things. I vividly remember being taught how to pray the *kiddish* (the blessings over food and drink) as well as the reciting of the four questions of the Passover, which explained the reasons Jews celebrate the holiday. Grand Pop Salter gave me the specific responsibility of reciting the questions in Hebrew. This is typical in Jewish homes as a means to encourage children to become involved in the Seder.

As a young boy, I had mixed feelings in a few respects when it came to the eight-day Feast of Passover and Unleavened Bread. At one level it gave me a sense of identity as a Jewish boy. On another however, it felt terribly restrictive especially when it came to food. I remember the special candies designated kosher for Passover, but somehow they did not taste as good. The restrictions aside, the celebrations were meaningful even to one who was very young.

Hebrew School

When I was eleven years old Grand Pop Salter enrolled me in Hebrew School. The Sons of Jacob synagogue, like many other synagogues, used this educational format to accomplish two main objectives. The first was to educate young Jewish boys concerning what it meant to be Jewish. This included a brief survey of the highlights of the Old Testament along with the cultural implications of Judaism. The highlights were the stories of God's great victories on behalf of His chosen people. Included among these were the miracles of the ten plagues and the crossing of the Red Sea, the victory of David over the Philistine giant Goliath, and the preservation of the Jews through Esther during the period of exile. Curiously, there was never any mention of Israel's prolonged periods of disobedience and idolatry.

The second principle objective of Hebrew School in the lives of young Jewish boys was to prepare them for their Bar Mitzvah (lit. *son of commandment*). The Bar Mitzvah is a coming-to-manhood rite for Jewish boys that traditionally takes place within the context of their thirteenth birthday. In Orthodox Judaism, Jewish boys are given the honor of reading the assigned passage from the Torah (the Law) during the Sabbath service that corresponds to the day the Bar Mitzvah is celebrated. Because it is desired that this be done in the original language of the text, boys must be taught to read Hebrew, a not-so-easy task. Hebrew School teaches young boys to read Hebrew for their Bar Mitzvah and hopefully beyond as they learn to become observant Jews.

In my situation, I attended Hebrew School after regular school hours. My father picked me up at the conclusion of his workday, typically shortly after five o'clock. As I remember, I attended two or three times a week. While the classes were tiring at the end of a long school day, they were not unpleasant experiences. My teacher was nice and tried to make the process of learning history and language interesting. He would, at times, make learning Hebrew fun by playing games like "Hebrew Baseball," something which I would obviously connect with. In the game, we would read a passage of the Torah in Hebrew as fast and with as few mistakes as possible. At the end of a specified time, depending upon how fast we read and how many mistakes we made, we would either hit a single, double, triple, home run, or make an out. Each student would represent his team for an at bat (half an inning). When nine innings were completed, the game was over. Needless to say, this made the roughly two hours go by very quickly.

Sometimes we would take part in plays for the entire synagogue during certain holidays. On one occasion, I remember having a part in a play during Purim. Purim is a holiday that celebrates the deliverance of the Jews from an attempt by Haman, an evil high official of the Persian Empire, to exterminate them. The miraculous deliverance took place during the period of Jewish captivity. The story of Purim is found in the Book of Esther.

In the play, I only had two lines, but I recall them vividly.

I was one of King Ahasuerus's royal advisors. The context of my part in the play was the story found in the first chapter of the Book of Esther. In the account, Queen Vashti refused to be paraded before the king's royal officials and subsequently embarrassed the king before his nobles. Since this left him humiliated, he asked his advisors for counsel. My part in the first act was to advise a response. I was the first to offer advice. "I'd take away all her powder, rouge, lipstick, and mirrors. Boy, would she like that!" was my two cents. Esther's account reveals that the king eventually opted for a harsher punishment—permanent banishment from his presence and loss of her royal position as queen (Esther 1:19–20).

More important to my ultimate spiritual journey were my remembrances of questions asked of the teacher during discussion times. Two questions stood out. One was, "Why do Jewish people not believe in Jesus?" I remember the essence of the teacher's answer. It was something to the effect that Jews believe Jesus was a good moral teacher, but only a man. It was therefore deeply wrong to believe that he was God, because there is only one God as stated in the Old Testament Shema which states, "Hear O Israel: The LORD our God, the LORD is one" (Deuteronomy 6:4)."

The second question I remember was a compound one. "Do Jews believe in heaven and hell, and if so, how can we go to heaven?" Again, I can distinctly recall our teacher's reply. First, he stated that the Old Testament was vague about the reality of an afterlife. He added that if there was indeed life hereafter, Jews believe that God would judge each person by balancing their mitzvahs (good deeds and obedience to the divine commandments) with bad deeds. If the balance was in the person's favor, they could expect a reward. If not, the opposite expectation could apply.

Why these questions stood out to me is a part of the divine

mystery concerning how God calls people to himself. I believe that He was planting the seeds of questions that I would ultimately pursue more earnestly. They would become very important as I would increasingly engage painful situations and difficult challenges.

Shabbat

Although Hebrew School left some lasting impressions, my understanding of what it meant to be a Jew was largely modeled by my grandfather. Grand Pop Salter was an Orthodox Jew, which essentially meant that he followed an approach to Judaism that emphasized following the Torah in ways prescribed in the Talmud. The Talmud is a series of oral traditions, rabbinic opinions and teachings of literally thousands of rabbis on a large number of subjects related to the Torah, ethics, and numerous issues relating to Jewish life. Grand Pop Salter was deeply respected by members of the Sons of Jacob synagogue as an elder. He sought to follow the precepts of Orthodox Judaism and pass them on to me, his grandson.

An important part of Jewish orthodoxy relates to the keeping of the Sabbath. As stated previously, Jews celebrate the Sabbath from sunset Friday evening to sunset on Saturday, since in Jewish thinking, a day begins at evening. Orthodox Jews take abstinence from all work very seriously since it was the Fourth Commandment given by God to Moses on Mount Sinai. The commandment instructed God's people to "Remember the Sabbath day by keeping it holy" (Exodus 20:8).

How one keeps the Sabbath holy or separate is a matter of question that can be answered differently through different perspectives, however. Orthodox Jews follow the dictates of the oral rabbinic traditions, which prescribe which acts are specifically allowed and which are disallowed. My grandfather followed them strictly. He would among other things, engage in no business, carry no money in his pocket, lift no object that exceeded a certain amount of weight, and not ride in a car or walk a distance that was not accepted by these traditions. Neither would he turn on any electric appliance nor use the telephone, since these too were considered "work" or common activity engaged in on other days.

I noted earlier that one exception to this came in his later years when he became increasingly frail. Because walking to the synagogue became more and more difficult, he would ride with a somewhat less-Orthodox friend who would park around the corner of the synagogue and walk the last block. Not only was it considered disrespectful to drive up to the door, an observant Jew would not want to advertise any compromise to recognized accepted behavior, even though in my grandfather's situation, it would have been understood.

I did not always attend the synagogue on the Sabbath because my father and mother were not observant. They seldom attended. Neither did my grandmother, not because she was not observant—she had to be in order to be married to my grandfather—but because in Orthodox Judaism, attendance by the women in the family was not required or expected. When I did attend, of course it was with Grand Pop Salter. He would proudly introduce me to members of the synagogue as his grandson. He would give me a *yamulka* (skull cap), and I would watch him pray the prescribed prayers in Hebrew while he rocked back and forth, tapping his chest in typical Orthodox fashion.

After some time I became known at the Sons of Jacob as Isaac and Rose Salter's grandson. My grandmother was active in the sisterhood of the synagogue and very much a part of the congregation, even though she, like most women, did not regularly attend services. I loved my grandparents and respected them greatly as I watched them practice their faith. They were always proud of me and stated that over and again.

A Community of Learning and Life

The synagogue is essentially a community of instruction and relationships. It seeks to provide all that is necessary to keep Jewish identity in the hearts of its people. In that respect, synagogues serve very similar roles as churches do for Christian believers. Daily and weekly prayer services are accompanied by a number of different annual gatherings that either highlight historic and current Jewish culture or simply provide opportunities for families to interact and enjoy life.

At the Sons of Jacob, people celebrated the Bar Mitzvahs of their sons and the Bat Mitzvahs (daughter of the commandment) of their daughters. Girls in Orthodox Jewish communities had similar celebrations although they did not publicly take part in formal services, as did the boys. Synagogue communities provided opportunities to share in weddings and circumcisions, as well as picnics and numerous other educational and cultural events. Some of these our immediate family participated in and others we did not. When we did participate, it was usually just Alice and me along with Grandma and Grand Pop Salter. Mom and Dad typically stayed home.

I don't remember thinking much about Mom and Dad's lack of participation. In retrospect, it was clear that they were not very social. It was also the case that they had little interest in what went on at the Sons of Jacob. Synagogue life was, in our minds, the exclusive domain of my grandmother and grandfather. I guess Mom and Dad just felt out of place.

Looking back, the Sons of Jacob forged a sense of the existence of God within me. It was mixed together with a strong emphasis on Jewish identity, but it was real nonetheless. The concept of God was deep in my consciousness. Instinctively, I knew that I was accountable to Him. My mind was very aware that there was a Judge in heaven that I would one day meet.

Chapter 3

Baseball and the Bond between a Father and Son

"Do you not know that in a race all the runners run, but only one gets the prize? Run in such a way as to get the prize."
—1 Corinthians 9:24

"Love is the most important thing in the world, but baseball is pretty good, too."
—Yogi Berra

I remember my incredible disappointment. It had rained all morning, but we were hopeful nonetheless. By the time we left for Philadelphia and Connie Mack Stadium, the rain had subsided. Dad and I were on our way, just the two of us. I had my baseball glove on my left hand and my Phillies cap covering my head and part of my forehead. Nothing was more special than going to see the Phighten Phils play in real life, especially with Dad.

But as we arrived at Twenty-first and Lehigh Avenue where Connie Mack Stadium stood, we saw the sign. "No Game Today. Cancelled Because of Rain." Dad assured me that we could get a rain check that would enable us to attend another game with the ticket stubs for the rained out one, but that didn't help much. My heart was set on watching the Phillies play and that would have to wait for another time.

As noted earlier, much of what makes up our stories is what we often regard as seemingly irrelevant detail. I say, "seemingly irrelevant detail," because so much of it is not as irrelevant as we think. What is typically passed off as the detail that fills in the main events is actually very important to who we are. If we take enough time to reflect, we will likely find that many of the realities in our lives are directly traceable to experiences in our pasts. This is clearly true in my life as it relates to my deep love for the game of baseball. While it may seem to be an unusual detour from the story of my journey to Christ, nonetheless this devotion was and is an integral part of my remembrance.

What makes baseball in general and the Philadelphia Phillies in particular significant in my life is that they comprise an extremely important aspect in my memory of my father. What happened to Dad deeply impacted my life for many years, and in some ways still does. It is hard to think of him apart from these fond and related memories. Whatever the reasons, the two have become inseparable.

The Philadelphia Phillies or "Phighten Phils," as they are often affectionately called, have the distinction of being the oldest, continuing one-city, one-name team in the history of American professional sports. They also have the distinction of being the team that has lost the most games in sports history, by far. This reality is only partially related to their being the oldest franchise. Historically speaking, they have been very, very bad. In a period covering more than 130 years, the Phillies have won only seven National League pennants, with only two of these resulting in their winning the coveted World Series.

I can remember Dad cheering for the Phillies from the time

I was about six years old. With devotion, he would tell stories of Richie Ashburn, Robin Roberts, Jim Konstanty, Del Ennis, Granny Hamner and other players from the beloved "Whiz Kids" who had won the team's second-ever National League pennant at the time and its first since 1915. Never mind that these 1950 Phillies lost four straight to the mighty New York Yankees in the World Series. The team made up of a significant number of young players came out of nowhere to overcome years of baseball futility and will forever live in Phillies' lore. This would turn out to be a very brief period of success, however. The "Phightens" returned to their frustration and their typical place as cellar dwellers shortly afterwards. During the late '50s and '60s, the Phillies were associated by most observers with baseball futility.

Phillies fans are a notoriously hardy band of sports enthusiasts. Undoubtedly, the same can also be said about fans of a few other sports franchises. Similar claims can also be made for Cubs and Red Sox fans since they too have endured very long extended periods of disappointment. But they are not my teams and do not fit into my personal story. Sports are no different than other aspects of life in one respect—difficulties can make you hardy and resolute.

The 1964 Season

It wouldn't be until 1964 that the Phils would offer a real challenge for the National League pennant. Just like the 1950 club, it came seemingly out of nowhere. While the team showed significant improvement the prior year, few thought they would be legitimate contenders in '64. As a young boy, this is where baseball intersects with my story. My memories of the "Phighten Phils" would include the names Dick (Richie) Allen, Johnny Callison, Tony Taylor, Cookie Rojas,

Jim Bunning, and Chris Short. Like Dad, I had few experiences with rooting for a winner (actually in my case, I had none), but in 1964 all that appeared to change.

Fathers and sons are meant to bond and such bonding can occur in a great variety of ways. For some, it takes place when they take time to go fishing in a lake or stream. For others, it happens when a father teaches his son to hunt with a gun or bow. Still others grow close through the teaching of carpentry or other skills. I did none of these things with Dad. But Dad and I grew close through a love for a baseball team. He taught me to be a fan of a team through thick and thin. Unfortunately for Dad and me, it was nearly always thin.

In 1964, it appeared that this was about to change. The Phillies were in first place from the beginning of the season. They seemed destined to win their first pennant in my lifetime. I was twelve years old, born two years after Dad's treasured "Whiz Kids" shocked the baseball world. I remember going to a game during the '64 season and the Phillies winning. I remember listening to parts of games and waking up happy because they won. The idea of them being a winning team was altogether new and exciting. As the season progressed, every indication was that this was going to be the Phillies' year.

Dad and I would not only root for the Phillies to win, we would follow the team statistically. We would take turns reading the sports sections of the Philadelphia papers, giving special attention to the Phillies' box scores. We knew who was hitting well and who was in a slump. We knew who was pitching consistently and who was unreliable. I remember Dad teaching me about important nuances of a baseball lineup and why Phillies manager Gene Mauch platooned his players, starting left-handed hitters against right-handed pitchers and vice versa. The Phillies were a huge part of our relationship, and during most of the 1964 season, it was way more fun than usual. After all, 1964 seemed certain to be the Phillies' year.

On one memorable Sunday afternoon, June 21st on Father's Day in fact, I went to the annual Sons of Jacob picnic at Alliance Beach in Norma, New Jersey. My sister, grandparents. and I (Mom and Dad stayed home as usual because it was a Sons of Jacob event) were enjoying ourselves swimming in the Maurice River and eating our favorite picnic foods when I heard the radio blaring in the background. It was the Phillies and New York Mets playing the first game of a doubleheader. Jim Bunning was pitching and pitching well. As time went on, the Phils' announcer "By" Saam made clear that Bunning was getting increasingly close to pitching the first National League perfect game since 1880. When the game reached the ninth inning, it seemed that everyone had gathered around to listen to every out. When Bunning struck out Johnny Stephenson of the Mets for the final out, everyone cheered. He had just pitched the first National league perfect game in eighty-four years. Dad described the entire game to me when I got home and we relived it together. It sure seemed like the Phillies' year.

Another great memory that year was the All Star Game. One of the three Phillies' All Star representatives was outfielder Johnny Callison. He came up in the bottom of the ninth inning with the score tied. He proceeded to hit a walk-off, three-run home run. There has not been an All Star Game that has ended in quite the same way since. In my life, I had never witnessed a Phillie as an All Star Game hero. It sure seemed like the Phillies' year.

The 1964 season was becoming a day-after-day celebration for Dad and me, at least from the perspective of a twelve-year-old. At times we sat in the back of the auto parts store listening to the occasional day games. On other occasions, we would listen to the first five or six innings of a night game in Dad's car until he made me get ready for bed. On summer evenings, I was allowed to stay up a little later and enjoy another inning or two of what more often than not turned into a Phillies win. Unfortunately, the final month of the season would prove to be the most memorable.

The last month of the season opened with the "Phightens" in first place with a five-and-a-half game lead. During the first three weeks of the month, they played well increasing their lead to six-and-a-half games. *Sports Illustrated* even photographed Jim Bunning with the intent of putting his picture on the cover of their World Series edition. *TV Guide* began printing their World Series preview featuring a photo of Connie Mack Stadium, the Phillies' ballpark. The National League had given the team permission to print World Series tickets. After all, they were in first place with a six-and-a-half game lead and there were only twelve games left to play. No team in the long history of the game of baseball had given up such a lead with so few games left. It seemed certain that this was the Phillies' year.

Then the unthinkable happened. The Phillies began to lose. They lost and lost and kept on losing. What was even worse, the Reds and Cardinals, the two teams closest to the Phillies in the standings, started winning. Dad and I kept thinking, "They'll win tomorrow," but each tomorrow they lost. When the dust had settled, the Phillies had lost ten in a row and had fallen behind the St. Louis Cardinals and Cincinnati Reds into third place. Entering the last weekend of the season, their situation was virtually hopeless. They were two-and-a-half games behind the Cards and two games behind the Reds. Loyal Phillies fans, and the entire baseball world for that matter, were in a state of shock.

While I remember much of the '64 baseball season, it was the final weekend that I remember most vividly. The Phillies and Reds played each other on Friday and Sunday during that last weekend. For some odd reason each was off on Saturday, a real fluke in the schedule. Meanwhile, the Cards had the great fortune of playing their last three games against the lowly last place Mets. The Mets had a miserable record of 51 wins and 108 losses going into that last weekend and were universally considered to be the worst team in all of baseball. St. Louis' record going into their final three games by contrast was 92 wins and 67 losses. The situation was surely hopeless. The Phillies, who were in the midst of the ten-game losing streak, had only one chance. They had to beat the red hot Reds twice, while the equally red hot Cardinals had to lose all three games to baseball's worst team.

Baseball can be a very strange game. Of the combined final five games, I still remember the scores of four of them: 4 to 3, 1 to 0, 15 to 5, and 10 to 0. I remember Dad walking into my bedroom Saturday morning of that final weekend and telling me that the Phils had broken their ten-game losing streak and had beaten the Reds 4 to 3. Not only that, but the Mets, behind their best pitcher, shut out the Cards 1 to 0. At least going into Saturday, there was still some hope, not much mind you, but some.

Saturday featured only one game. The Cardinals and the Mets were to play in the afternoon. When afternoon came, I sat by my radio listening for some news outlet to give the score. When it came I was astounded. The Mets had beaten St. Louis 15 to 5. With one game left for the Cardinals, Reds, and Phillies, the Cardinals and Reds were tied for first place with the Phillies one game back. All that needed to happen was for the Phillies to beat the Cincinnati Reds and the Mets to beat St. Louis one more time. It was improbable, but considering what had taken place the two previous days, it was at least not as improbable as it had been.

Dad and I hoped for a miracle on Sunday. We listened to the Phillies-Reds game and the news was good. The Phillies were thumping the Reds 10 to 0. We had to wait a while for the Cards-Mets score. The news was bad. St. Louis was winning big. They eventually won the game and this twelve-year-old boy was heartbroken. Oddly enough but perhaps not surprisingly, the Cards-Mets final score is the only one that has not been etched in my memory.

I cannot say what Dad felt after that final day of the 1964 season. I assume he was used to such disappointments when it came to his favorite baseball team. But for a twelve-year-old boy, it was a crushing, empty feeling. I can only assume my sadness was shared by many fathers and sons and mothers and daughters, for that matter. That '64 season has been dubbed by many as the greatest collapse in baseball history. In the years that followed, it has been called "the great phold," and the team gained the infamous name the "Phizz Kids," to contrast with the dearly loved 1950 Whiz Kids.

That night a dad comforted his son with the hope that next year would be better. Next year however would not turn out to be better. It would be far worse, but not for reasons related to baseball. My life would take a tragic turn in 1965, one that would change its direction in more ways than I even now understand. The memory of my dad comforting me that Sunday night was to be the last significant memory I have of my father.

Chapter 4

A Tragic Turning Point

"When you pass through the waters, I will be with you;
and when you pass through the rivers,
they will not sweep over you.
When you walk through the fire, you will not be burned;
the flames will not set you ablaze."
—Isaiah 43:2

"The tragedy of life is what dies inside a man while he lives"
—Albert Schweitzer

I began the year 1965 with great anticipation. In January, I turned thirteen years of age. For a Jewish boy, turning thirteen is a big deal. It meant Bar Mitzvah, and Bar Mitzvah meant manhood. It also meant gifts—lots and lots of gifts. This would even be true for a Jewish boy from a relatively poor family. You see, gifts would come from all over. They would come from family members, members of the Sons of Jacob synagogue, and others. A Bar Mitzvah is a big, big deal.

On the Sabbath just before my birthday, I was to be the designated reader of the passage of the Torah at the Sons of Jacob synagogue. The passage was a couple of paragraphs in length and would require a flawless enunciation of the Hebrew text.

It should be noted that reading Hebrew does not require an understanding of what one is reading, but it is difficult, nonetheless. Jewish boys are taught to enunciate correctly because the entire congregation, including many relatives would be watching and listening.

When the day of my Bar Mitzvah finally arrived, I was fully prepared. The rabbi called me forward as he would a grown man and gave me the honor of reading from the sacred scroll. My nervousness was evident to me as I sat in my seat awaiting the moment, but to my surprise, I read the passage calmly and flawlessly. After doing so, I remember proudly returning to my seat with the eyes of the congregation fixed upon me.

On the following day, a party was held in the house of Grandma and Grand Pop Salter in my honor. My extended family on my mother's side was all there. Most of them came from Philadelphia, where most of my maternal relatives lived. As far as I can remember, only Dad was present from his side of the family. They were very nominal and many lived farther away. Some members of Sons of Jacob also came with gifts. It was a day of honor and family celebration.

Oddly enough, while Mom and Dad were there, I don't have vivid impressions of them. My most clear remembrances are of Grandma and Grand Pop Salter. Perhaps this is because it was a much more important occasion to them. Strangely or perhaps not so, it seems that my most clear recollections of Dad revolve around baseball, while those of my grandparents have to do with my Jewish training.

I now understand that my parents did not have a great relationship. Lots of things become obvious retrospectively that you do not perceive when you are a child. Children tend to block out the circumstances that have the potential to threaten their security. For instance, I recall that later in my childhood, Dad slept in my room rather than with Mom. I remember he used his bad back as an excuse. The change in where he slept escaped my concern at the time, but now I recognize that it was symptomatic of problems in their relationship.

Sorrow upon Sorrow

Sometime during 1964, Dad's job situation changed. My Uncle Herman decided to close the Vineland auto parts store and open a new location in Pleasantville, New Jersey, nearly an hour's drive away. From what I came to understand later, Dad's pay didn't increase however. I don't know whether or not he was compensated for the additional travel expenses, but I do know that this increased commuting responsibility put additional pressure on him. I specifically remember him being increasingly anxious over finances. On at least one occasion, Dad had to borrow money from his brother-in-law, my Uncle Ned, his sister Mildred's husband.

One day early in March 1965, I remember sitting on our living room couch waiting for Dad to get home. This was a typical routine of mine. Dad often brought something home when he returned from a day of work. He usually pulled his 1954 Plymouth into the driveway about six in the evening. I could usually hear the car when it was one or two houses away.

This early March evening would be different, however. Dad did not arrive as scheduled. After a couple of hours Mom became concerned enough to call Uncle Herman and ask if he knew where Dad was. Uncle Herman said he left the Pleasantville store at the regular closing time. He added with a little hesitation that they had argued before he left. He urged Mom to call him when Dad arrived.

But Dad did not arrive. I remember shortly after Mom's conversation with Uncle Herman that she called the police. They arrived late that evening and asked her a battery of questions concerning Dad's recent actions, and whether or not she had noticed a change in attitude and emotional outlook. As my sister Alice and I listened intently, I remember becoming more and more afraid. There was an instinctive feeling that things were very, very wrong. I worked hard to put my fears out of my mind and, in typical childhood fashion, was somewhat successful. At about eleven or twelve that night, I went to bed convincing myself that my father would be home by morning.

When I woke up the next morning, the first thing I did was check to see if Dad had arrived, but Mom said he hadn't. Grandma and Grand Pop Salter had traveled to Florida as they typically did each winter. They weren't scheduled to return for another month or two. The only thing I could think of doing was taking my place on the living room sofa and hope that he would somehow arrive with an explanation. Maybe, I thought, he stayed at a motel for a night to clear his head. Maybe, he would take a few days to think things through and then come home. I would do the only thing I could—sit in my traditional place on the sofa—and wait.

Waiting however would do no good. The days went by and there was no word. After some time, word got around the neighborhood. Dad was listed by the city police as "missing" since his status was unknown. While much of March 1965 is a giant blur in my memory, I remember some things clearly. As time went on, two things took place. Outwardly, Mom, Alice, and I would project the belief that Dad would return eventually with some explanation of the events that caused his disappearance. Deep within however, at least in my heart, there was a growing loss of hope and deepening fear.

One day, about two or three weeks after my father's disappearance, our Orthodox Jewish neighbors Herb and Al Behrig saw me outside my house and asked if there was any word about my dad. I responded that we thought he might be in Philadelphia. I said this partially because we speculated that this was possible, but mostly because I did not know what else to say. They didn't press me further, but I suspect that they didn't put much credence in my answer.

Looking back, my remembrance of March 1965 was largely characterized by a nagging dread. Somehow, Alice and I went to school and kept a relatively normal schedule. Alice was in the tenth grade and I was in the seventh. Mom simply sat home, repressing her fears. Each afternoon I would come home and wait, usually taking my place on the sofa around 6 p.m., hoping that this one day would be different from the others, with Dad pulling in the driveway and everything okay again.

All our hopes were dashed one Saturday afternoon in early April when a city policeman arrived at the door. I was in the kitchen. Mom and Alice were in the living room. I remember the look on his face. It was solemn and expressionless. As he walked in the door, he said he had news. In my heart at that moment, I knew Dad was dead. Trembling, I listened as he gave us the details in response to Mom's repeated questions. Dad was found in a wooded area outside of the city of Pleasantville. Two children had stumbled upon his body while playing. He had a plastic bag over his head. It was surmised that he had taken his own life by suffocating himself.

Even now more than fifty years later, as I contemplate this event, a rush of deep sadness causes me to stop and ponder. It is still, after all this time, very painful. It is not surprising that I would find myself emotionally blocking it out for many years. We often think that we have gotten over traumatic events, only to realize that they are still in our consciousness. They impact us in a variety of ways, most of which we are unaware of. Trauma is like that. I have heard it said that our minds develop a form of scar tissue, similar to our bodies. When we are cut, our bodies form a barrier to protect the wound. Perhaps something similar takes place in our minds, protecting us from the pain of our lives and blocking out the memories that are the most painful.

When the policeman gave us the terrible news, I do not recall crying. I just stood there numb, not saying a word. Mom and Alice cried, but I didn't. It is possible that the horrible news was a confirmation of a reality already emotionally processed. It is also possible that it was my way of shutting my emotions off.

Dad's funeral, like most Jewish funerals, took place as soon as possible after death. I remember staring at his closed casket and suddenly becoming overcome with emotion. I recall screaming, shaking, and having to be restrained. It took some time for my relatives to calm me down. Other than vague images of a family gathering afterwards, I have no additional recollections of the funeral.

The tragic events of spring 1965 however were not limited to the loss of my father. We received news from Grandma Salter that Grand Pop had died suddenly of a heart attack in Florida. While in the synagogue he attended during the winter months, Grand Pop Salter had been given the honor of lifting the Torah scroll and placing it on the bench to be tied and covered. Typically, a man would bend his knees, take the scroll by the handles, and lift it because the scroll was relatively heavy and another man or boy (over thirteen years of age) would bind the scroll and place the covering over it. Grand Pop, who was seventy-six years old, had a heart attack while lifting the scroll and collapsed on the bench where the Torah was placed. He died the next day.

The Immediate Aftermath

For a thirteen-year-old boy, the first task is to find a new sense of normalcy in life following a tragedy. In my case, among other things, it meant that after a week or so, I would have to return to school. More than anything, I wanted to be a normal thirteen-year-old boy again. I wanted to have friends, play sports, and just be a typical kid, doing what typical kids do.

The requirements of Orthodox Judaism and the expectations of family and the Sons of Jacob congregation would make that difficult. While Jews observe their mourning obligations in varying degrees, the prescribed requirements are very specific. Included among other things are the following: (1) Shiva (seven)–a seven-day period of mourning where the family stays home; (2) *Shloshim* (thirty)–a thirty-day period (including Shiva) where festive occasions are avoided; and (3) *Shneim asar chodesh* (twelve months)–a twelve-month period (including *Shloshim*) where the oldest son regularly recites what is called the mourner's kaddish during the regular synagogue services, as often as possible.

In my case, I had the immediate requirement after Shiva, of avoiding fun activities for thirty days. More difficult, however, was the requirement of wearing a black ribbon on my shirt to depict my state of mourning. Each day, I would be asked numerous times why I was wearing the ribbon and I would have to explain that my father died. Occasionally, I would be asked how he died and I would not know how to respond. So I would just make something up.

As difficult as the period surrounding Dad's suicide was for Alice and me individually, it was in some respects much more so for Mom. Mom became emotionally fractured and rather than take any leadership, she gradually withdrew into her own thoughts, leaving Alice and me to mostly fend for ourselves. I can only speculate when it comes to why Mom responded the way she did. Perhaps there was some layer of guilt over the state of their marriage immediately before Dad's suicide. Guilt can do devastating things to people.

Looking back, there was little conversation about anything important in our family in the time after the dual tragedies. Each of us began the process of retreating into our own worlds and dealing with our new circumstances in the best ways we could. Our thoughts, feelings, and personal struggles were our own. None of us had anyone with whom we could really talk.

Despite her own personal loss, there was one person who was a constant strength in our family during this time—Grandma Salter. She had a deep internal strength. I do not know where it came from, but we always knew she was someone upon whom we could rely. Grandma could be dominating at times, but considering how fragile our family was, her strong will was often a necessity. Not only was she an important resource, we all recognized that she loved us very much. Her house was in a different part of the city and because no one in the family drove (Mom and Grandma never learned to drive, and Alice and I were too young at the time), her influence often came from a distance.

Unfortunately, when the storms of life come to people, they often are unable to cope. It is common for people in pain to blame themselves, others, or both. Tragedy will either pull people together or drive them apart. In the case of our extended family, those who desired to be a resource were too far away and those who were close and able to help seemed to get caught up in the blame game. Dad's brother, Uncle Herman, and his wife Edith in all likelihood struggled as well. I do not remember them ever stopping by to find out how we were or even calling on the phone. Perhaps it was too painful. Maybe they did not know what to say to us. I guess when all was said and done, Mom, Alice, and I were not the only ones who retreated into their own worlds.

The year 1965 became a real watershed year for me and virtually every other close relative in my family. Its ripples influenced the course of our lives. Feelings of guilt, shame, and remorse along with the kind of isolation and loneliness that commonly accompany such feelings would dominate for some time. Tragedy often does that.

Chapter 5
Blame, Separation, and Dysfunction

"The words of the reckless pierce like swords, but the tongue of the wise brings healing."
—Proverbs 12:18

"If only Pearl was a better wife to him . . . if only Herman paid him more money." Blame, deflection, accusation . . . that's the way I recall how my extended family dealt with the awful circumstances of my father's suicide. "It's *his/her* fault this happened, not *mine*." We were all in pain.

It hurts when someone you love is taken from you. It hurts even more when it didn't have to happen. Someone has to be considered responsible, we reasoned. In the end, blame only compounded the pain we were experiencing.

Maybe it was in some way my fault, I feared, as I pondered the ever-present "Why?" After all, why wasn't I enough to keep this from happening? I thought Dad and I were very close. We shared a special father-son bond. I was convinced of it. Did Dad love me as much as I thought? Could I have done something, anything to prevent this?

While it is true that dysfunction begins with painful

thoughts and feelings, it becomes enflamed by words. Contrary to the old rhyme "Sticks and stones may break my bones, but words will never hurt me," words not only hurt, but they endure long past the physical harm of mere broken bones. They also typically metastasize to cause even greater harm.

Estrangement

Humanity's fallen condition more often than not will add further complication to what are already deeply painful circumstances. The prospect of accepting what might be one's responsibility for events that take place is too difficult for many to bear. It becomes far easier to blame others for these events and attempt to absolve ourselves of any significant responsibility. The world is full of families whose members are estranged from one another because of their responses to tragic events. Most of the time, animosities are never overcome.

As I intimate in the previous chapter, that is precisely what would ultimately take place in the Jaffe extended family. Before I go on, I would like to say I have long since let go of any desire to attach blame over whatever caused my father's decision to take his life. My Uncle Herman, Aunt Edith, Mom, and most others have long since passed away. In fact, I do not remember attaching any blame in the immediate aftermath of Dad's passing anyway. At the time, I was most preoccupied with my way forward, so preoccupied that there was little time for anything else in my thought processes.

My simple goal in this chapter is to as dispassionately as possible comment on what took place and why. In so doing, I want to express how it was a deeply unfortunate reality, one that doubtless affected us all. None of us were able to receive any consolation from other members of the family, which could have helped us as we sought to look to a future.

With the exception of my Aunt Mildred and her family, there was no contact that I could recall from anyone on my father's side of the family. Uncle Herman and Aunt Edith had two children, Susan and Bob, who were older than Alice and me. My vague remembrance is that their family blamed Mom for Dad's suicide and that Mom blamed them. I would like to state again that this kind of thing happens because people try to make sense of tragedies. It has only been within the last couple of years that I have learned that my cousins are still alive. My hope is that someday I will have the opportunity to connect with them.

I cannot know this for a fact, but it would not surprise me if early on my Uncle Herman picked up the phone on a couple of occasions or perhaps started to write a letter but did not follow through. After time it probably became harder and harder to know where or how to originate some contact. Eventually, perhaps he gave up and rationalized that it would not be productive to contact us. That tends to be the way things like this work. In the end, there would be no further relationship whatsoever between Mom, Alice, and me and most of the Jaffe side of the family.

Dysfunction and Isolation

Our isolation from the rest of the Jaffe clan was the least of our problems during those days however. The largest and most debilitating problem faced by my mother, my sister, and me was what took place within the walls of our home. Mom became increasingly dysfunctional by retreating within herself. Alice and I had to struggle through what we perceived to be Mom's seemingly constant nagging and virtually nonexistent parental guidance. That Mom also was experiencing terrible pain unfortunately did not appear on my radar. I cannot speak for Alice, but I felt almost entirely on my own when it came to my development.

It would become clear to me early on, that my journey through adolescence would take place all by myself. There would be no one to talk to when I would have questions about important things. There would be no one to discuss my physiological, emotional, and social struggles. My adolescence would be devoid of a single male figure to guide me. As a result, beginning at the age of thirteen, I would largely make my own decisions. During the years that followed, I would make bad choices that would complicate my life. God intended young boys to have fathers, and I was among those who would be deprived of that benefit.

In addition to lacking a father figure and at least partially as a result of it, I would experience another unrelenting reality. My teenage years would be characterized by intense feelings of loneliness or, maybe more accurately stated, feelings of aloneness. These feelings would often be accompanied by a number of fears—fear of the present, fear of the future, and even fear of dying.

This was a lot for a thirteen-year-old. I don't want to leave the impression that these feelings were constant. They were not. They were intermittent in the first couple of years, but as time went on, they grew and led me to increasingly doubt the future. I would seek to find solace through friends, my private thoughts, and a relatively brief pursuit of God through Orthodox Judaism.

During the years following, I would also characterize my thinking as almost entirely self-directed. My thoughts were consumed with my wants and needs. I cannot recall concerning myself with how Mom or Alice were doing. I guess

I concluded that they would have to find their own way. In time, I would realize their struggles were as great as mine. It would be a long time however, before their needs would be something I recognized.

The First Couple of Years

On the surface, the first two years of my adolescence after Dad's death would appear not too different from that of an ordinary teenager. Like most teenagers, I had school friends, interests, and peer pressure. I played sports recreationally and followed my favorite sports teams, especially the Phillies and the Eagles. Occasionally, my friend George Booskos and his parents would invite me to go with them to an Eagles game in Philadelphia. That was a real treat for a young teenager who had no money or opportunity to go on his own.

I remember two occasions. While they sort of blend together in my recollection, there is one thing that sticks out apart from my general memory of these exciting opportunities. Each time I went with the Booskos family to see the Eagles play, one thing occurred prior to attending the games. The Booskos were Greek Orthodox and attended church in Philadelphia, which was almost an hour from Vineland. I guess there was no Greek Orthodox congregation closer. Before the game, we would attend service during the morning. I recall feeling very odd during the service. The service followed a liturgy that I did not understand. I did not want to bow and participate so I just sat there, occasionally standing while others went through the various worship activities.

While I liked football, basketball, and other sports, and enjoyed following the Philadelphia teams, my first love was still the Phillies. In this respect, I was a mirror image of Dad. I would follow them relentlessly and, in doing so, endure the ongoing frustration of being a devoted Phillies fan. In the mid-1960s, the "Phightens" were not terrible, but they began a slow and steady decline from their near-success of the 1964 season. Whatever their fate, I would be there cheering them on.

Apart from sports, a few additional things stand out in my memory. I remember professing no interest in the opposite sex during my early teen years. That would gradually change inwardly, but the truth was that I was scared to death of girls during these years and had no idea how to deal with the biological changes I was experiencing. I became the last holdout among my friends, only eventually giving in because my peers were increasingly ridiculing me over my professed lack of interest. My situation was complicated by the fact that I was awkward, had no nice clothes, and had very little self-confidence.

There is one other aspect of the first couple of years of my adolescence that provides some insight into how my life was taking shape. I assumed the role as the person in charge of my life. More times than not, I rejected any authority Mom claimed over me. An example of this was when I took most of the money I had in my bank account, money received from my Bar Mitzvah gifts, and bought our family's first color television. Back then, color televisions were new and expensive. Mom objected to my irresponsible act, but it didn't matter. I did what I wanted and that would increasingly become the pattern of my teenage years.

Financial Hardships

Our family's struggle was exacerbated by its difficult financial situation. Our only income was money we received from Social Security. Mom had no work skills, had never learned to drive, and was not emotionally capable of holding down a job. As a result, we lived off of the survivor's benefits she received from the government along with the checks Mom received for Alice and me as dependent children.

While there was food on the table and a roof over our heads, there was little else. I had a paper route for a short time when I was in the seventh grade, but I eventually determined that it did not make me enough money to be worth my time. Because Mom did not drive, we walked everywhere we needed to go. That was not a big deal since most things we needed were within walking distance. I walked a mile and a half to school and back, to my friends' houses, as well as occasionally to Grandma Salter's house who lived about two miles away.

Because there was little money left over for clothes, Grandma would take me to a Jewish merchant and buy me basic shirts, pants, and other necessary items. I remember standing next to her, embarrassed as she would dicker with the merchant over the cost of whatever she was purchasing. She would talk to him about how long she had known his family and why he should lower the price as a result of their respective family histories. Needless to say, these are the kind of experiences from which most thirteen-year-olds would like to be spared. While her methods were not what I would have chosen, Grandma understood her need to fill in the financial gaps and help us get by.

Looking back, I do not know how we would have made it through these difficult first couple of years without her. Grandma Salter, in her own unique and often overbearing way, was able to keep Mom and the family somewhat stable. Whether it was financial help or just making the necessary decisions that Mom was unable to make, Grandma established some needed sense of structure to our lives.

Throughout my teenage years, we just barely survived

financially. I do not regret these times in some ways. They help me to emotionally connect to those who are less fortunate in life. They also taught me how to persevere in the face of hard times. At a very early age, I learned how to live off of what I had and get by in circumstances that were challenging to say the least. On the other hand however, there were obviously occasions when I felt deprived of things that others had. Shabby clothes are the kind of things that tend to define you in your junior high years. They define you to your peers, your friends, and most importantly to yourself.

Chapter 6

Phase One: The Search for Meaning . . . Judaism

" 'Meaningless! Meaningless!' says the Teacher.
'Utterly meaningless! Everything is meaningless.' "
—Ecclesiastes 1:2

"If there is meaning in life at all,
then there must be meaning in suffering."
—Viktor E. Frankl

The search for life's meaning is often associated with college age students or adults, but in my case it came much earlier. It seems in retrospect that after the deaths of my father and grandfather, this search was almost a preoccupation. Tragedy can lead people in different directions. For some, it can lead to depression. For others, it can lead to bitterness or some form of escape. In my case, at least in the near term, it led me to seriously contemplate the matters of life and death in both constructive and destructive ways.

Mourner's *Kaddish*

Previously, I noted the expectations in Jewish families when it came to the period of mourning over the death of loved ones. The twelve-month period called *Shneim asar chodesh* calls upon the eldest surviving male in the immediate family to recite what is known in Judaism as the mourner's *kaddish* during synagogue services. For the most part, this is done sparingly if at all, but in my situation, there was a strong emotional need to pursue something that could possibly hold my life together. From the beginning, I resolved to fulfill this responsibility in an extraordinarily serious manner. I determined to attend synagogue services every morning and evening in order to offer mourner's *kaddish* for my father and grandfather. I did this for the entire yearlong period and never missed one service.

Orthodox Jews hold services each morning just after sunrise and each evening at sunset. The evening prayer services welcome the new day since in Jewish reckoning each day begins at sunset. Mourner's *kaddish* was always recited in Hebrew, but the meaning would not be understood by most Jews, because like me they more often than not were taught to read the Hebrew prayers without generally learning the meaning of what they were saying. The English translation of the mourner's *kaddish* recited repeatedly during specified times of the prayer service is as follows:

May His great Name grow exalted and sanctified
[Congregation: Amen.]
in the world He created and willed.
May He give reign to His kingship in your lifetimes and in your days,
and in the lifetimes of the entire Family of Israel,
swiftly and soon. Now say:

[Congregation: Amen. May His great Name be blessed forever and ever.]
Blessed, praised, glorified, exalted, extolled,
mighty, upraised, and lauded be the Name of the Holy One.
Blessed is He beyond any blessing and song,
praise, and consolation that are uttered in the world. Now say:
[Congregation: Amen.]
May there be abundant peace from Heaven
and life upon us and upon all Israel. Now say:
[Congregation: Amen.]
He who makes peace in His heights, may He make peace,
upon us and upon all Israel. Now say:
[Congregation: Amen.]

Every morning, the Behrig brothers who attended morning prayers before work would pick me up and take me to the Sons of Jacob synagogue. After prayers were over, I would walk three-quarters of a mile to school and arrive just in time for homeroom. In the evenings, I would walk nearly a mile from home to the synagogue because the Behrigs only went to the morning services.

Since I had gone through my Bar Mitzvah just a few months before, I could be counted as one of the minimum of ten men required before a service could commence. Jews term this requirement a *minyan* (Hebrew word literally meaning "count"). Many times finding ten men that were willing to attend daily prayers was difficult. Most Jews, even those who profess to be Orthodox will only attend on Friday evenings or Saturday mornings for Sabbath services. As a result, having a thirteen-year-old boy attend each morning and evening faithfully was an unexpected asset to the congregation's ability to hold the twice-daily services. During that period, I was without exaggeration the most dependable of all attendees.

My motivations for attending the synagogue so faithfully were varied. First of all, I considered praying *kaddish* for Dad and Grand Pop Salter a near-sacred duty. *Kaddish* is an ancient tradition among Jews and is meant as a loving act on the part of the son or close relative that enables the departed soul to somehow enter God's presence. My determination to be faithful to them and their memory was extremely important to me. If there was something I could do for them, I deeply desired to do it.

Beyond that desire, there were other motivations, both good and self-serving. I derived satisfaction knowing that I was respected by those adult men in the congregation for my commitment. It seemed as if a day would not go by without someone commenting on my unusual devotion to the memory of both my father and grandfather. I cannot overstate how rare this commitment was. Few grown men had shown such personal commitment, choosing rather to engage a regular worshipper as a substitute who would say the *kaddish* prayer for them, since they were unable or unwilling to be present. Such substitutions are a very common practice.

The praise I received from the men of the Sons of Jacob helped meet an important internal need. I grew in my desire to please others. In fact, I probably hungered for it. Children and adolescents have a great natural need for the praise of those who are closest to them, and I received very little of this in my teenage years. Therefore gaining the respect of these men was very significant to me.

Apart from my previously mentioned motives, one more stands out. Tragedy often causes people to ask questions and I had a few very serious ones. Who is God? What does He want from me? If there is a heaven, would I be good enough to go there? As I progressed through my teenage years, these questions would always be there, sometimes in the forefront of my thinking, other times in my subconscious thinking, but always there.

Prayer Shawls and Phylacteries

While limited in their ultimate ability to satisfy an adolescent seeking to understand God and life, the external emblems and aspects of my religion provided enough meaning for the time being. Orthodox Judaism requires certain symbolic items as part of worship. One of these is the prayer shawl or *tallit* in Hebrew, which literally means "cover." The *tallit* is worn by men over their outer clothes during morning prayers. Additionally it is worn throughout the entire day of Yom Kippur, the Day of Atonement.

The Old Testament does not specifically require the wearing of the prayer shawl, although it is presumed that people wore a covering during tabernacle worship. Numbers 15:37–41 records the specific command given to Moses.

> The Lord said to Moses, "Speak to the Israelites and say to them: 'Throughout the generations to come you are to make tassels on the corners of your garments, with a blue cord on each tassel. You will have these tassels to look at and so you will remember all the commands of the Lord, that you may obey them and not prostitute yourselves by chasing after the lusts of your own hearts and eyes. Then you will remember to obey all my commands and will be consecrated to your God. I am the Lord your God, who brought you out of Egypt to be your God. I am the Lord your God.' "

The *tallit* or prayer shawl is required of all men thirteen years old and older and is typically given to Jewish boys at their Bar Mitzvah. It is usually a white linen garment with horizontal black or dark blue stripes and knotted fringes attached to each of its four corners. I received mine on the occasion of my Bar Mitzvah and it became a part of the daily routine during this time of my life. I would leave my *tallit* under the bench where I typically sat each morning. Prior to beginning the Hebrew prayer readings required on that particular morning, I would place the *tallit* around my shoulders, as did all the men who were present.

A second article that was required during all morning prayers was the phylacteries or *tfilin* in Hebrew. The word *phylacteries* literally means to guard or protect. In Jewish culture it refers to the need to protect the mind and heart from evil. The phylacteries are small, black leather boxes that contain parchment inscribed with verses from the Torah. Jewish men wear these boxes on their foreheads and wrapped around their left arms. They are worn during weekday morning prayers only and are not required during evening prayers, Sabbath services, or on high holy days.

The basis for putting on phylacteries is found in God's commands to His people as recorded in Deuteronomy 6. This passage extends from that which is known as the *Shema* (Hebrew "hear").

> "Hear, O Israel: The LORD our God, the LORD is one. Love the LORD your God with all your heart and with all your soul and with all your strength. These commandments that I give you today are to be on your hearts. Impress them on your children. Talk about them when you sit at home and when you walk along the road, when you lie down and when you get up. Tie them as symbols on your hands and bind them

> on your foreheads. Write them on the doorframes of your houses and on your gates."
> Deuteronomy 6:4–9

I received a set of *tfilin* (phylacteries) at my Bar Mitzvah as well. Along with my *tallit*, I would leave them under my prayer bench and put them on just as did the other men in attendance. With my *yamulka* (skull cap) on my head, *tallit* over my shoulders, and my *tfilin* on my forehead and wrapped around my left arm, I would read the morning prayers in Hebrew and copy the prayer form and practices of those around me. Jewish men typically would *daven*. To *daven* was to sway and rock back and forth as the prayers were recited. I am sure it amused those who watched me in a good sort of way as they watched me mimic the desired form of prayer. It clearly pleased them, as I became a "disciple" of orthodoxy following the traditions of the historic faith.

As I attended the synagogue during morning prayers, in the evenings, and during the Sabbath, I received a sense of satisfaction on many levels. I believed that I was pleasing God. I also felt the approval of others that I respected. Lastly, there was a sense of meaning in it all for me, although I was not sure what that meaning was. I only know that my heart was desperately in search of something that would attach significance to my existence. For the time being, my daily engagement with my Jewish faith would provide enough to help me through the loneliness and emptiness that filled my life.

Law Keeping

In Orthodox Judaism, attending regular prayer services was only part of what was required. The main focus of orthodoxy was the regular keeping of the Torah as defined by the oral traditions laid down in the Talmud. The word *Talmud* literally means "instruction" or "learning." It is the basic text of the Jewish rabbis. In it, the Law or Torah is elaborated upon. It identifies how the rabbis interpret the various dos and don'ts of keeping the requirements of Judaism.

While ethics and morals are important to Orthodox Judaism, much of what it means to be a practicing Jew involves external actions or inactions. This is especially true when it comes to the Sabbath, the high holy days, and dietary laws. While the commandment only requires Jews to keep the Sabbath day holy or separate, the rabbis through their oral traditions defined what that meant. Keeping the Sabbath was an especially rigorous undertaking. Serious, practicing Orthodox Jews for instance would not, among other things, carry money, turn on or off any electrical appliance, drive or ride in an automobile, or even walk more than a prescribed distance.

One way to acquire a picture of how modern-day Orthodox Jews respond to the Sabbath is to consider the Pharisees of Jesus' day. The Pharisees of the first century are very much the ancestors of today's Orthodox Judaism. The term "Pharisee" literally means "separated one." The Jewish sect emerged around the second century BC as a counter to the priestly class. What began as a holiness movement degenerated into an overly legalistic attempt to define righteousness by external actions. Modern Orthodox Jews adopt the same approach in their attempts at pleasing God.

During this period of my adolescence, I was influenced by my neighbors the Behrigs and other adult men in the Sons of Jacob synagogue. I attempted to follow the rabbinic traditions partly to please them, but also partly because I thought such behavior pleased God. The truth is my desire was to please anyone and everyone if I could.

Then there was also the memory of Grand Pop Salter. Grandma Salter was pleased by my attention to Judaism. She encouraged me from a distance as she heard of my dedication from wives of the synagogue's members. At this point in my life, I was willing to do virtually anything to gain the respect of people.

There was one big impediment to my living as a strict and observant Jew however. Mom had little desire to conform to the requirements of Jewish orthodoxy. For her, the legalistic demands were much too cumbersome. Mom was not alone in this regard. Most Jews, whether they are Conservative or Reform, generally feel similarly. Unless Grandma was watching, Mom would live her life as she chose, at least within certain boundaries. Mom's more casual attitude created additional tension in our home during this relatively brief period. I would argue with her about what she ate and what she did on the Sabbath. None of this would change her though. While it did not affect me much, Mom's attitude made any attempt to live "righteously" much more complicated for me. In the end, I did my best without Mom's cooperation.

Spooks, Shadows, and Questions

One other clear memory of this period of my life involves my walks to and from the synagogue as I attended evening services. As I mentioned earlier, mourner's *kaddish* was also recited during evening prayers. I considered it my obligation to fulfill the requirement completely. In doing so, I sometimes felt as though I was distinguishing myself from others more orthodox than myself. The Behrig brothers, for instance, because of their work schedule were unable to attend evening prayers. They were kosher butchers and had a kosher meat business in Norma, New Jersey, about ten miles or so from Vineland. Other men were unable to attend for similar reasons.

Since a *minyan* (a quorum of ten men) was required to begin any service, my presence often meant the difference between having the service or not. In this regard, I was becoming increasingly valued. Faithfully, I would be there each evening, even though I had to walk nearly a mile each way in order to attend.

Walking home would prove to be no small challenge. Because the prayer services could not begin until sunset, which marked the beginning of the next day by Jewish reckoning, by the time the service was over, it was always dark. The neighborhoods I had to walk through to get home were not crime ridden by any means, but they were not the best of neighborhoods either. I often remember walking home very briskly because I was only thirteen years old and scared.

It seemed as though every evening my imagination would get the best of me. I would regularly hear sounds that in my anxious state would cause me to jump. I would also find myself afraid of shadows from streetlights and, at times, feel a presence that would agitate me. Each night I couldn't get home fast enough. As I approached my house, I breathed a sigh of relief.

Commonly, my walks home from the Sons of Jacob were times that I would think about those God questions I referred to previously. Who is God? Would I go to heaven if I died? How could I know for sure? My walks home would allow much time for those "meaning of life questions." Questions about God, life, and death would be with me in varying degrees of intensity throughout my teenage years. Sometimes they would preoccupy my thinking, at other times they would come and go. But they would always be there.

In many ways, my sense of aloneness was very intense

during my walks to and especially from the synagogue in the evenings. Unhealthy fears of death and dying were all too common. Occasionally, I would wonder whether or not each walk home would be my last. The fears and the questions seemed to go together. If I did die, would God think I was worthy of heaven? I had no idea.

Chapter 7

Finding Friends

"Two are better than one, because they have a good return for their labor: If either of them falls down, one can help the other up. But pity anyone who falls and has no one to help them up."
—Ecclesiastes 4:9

"I get by with a little help from my friends."
—John Lennon

Teenage years are a challenge for most people, but for me they were especially difficult. As the years went by, I began doing a great deal of compartmentalization. I ultimately ended up coping by placing the tragedy in a room and throwing away the key. It would become my secret, something that no new person in my life would know. It became a part of my past from which I wanted to run.

These years were all about finding my way. Early on, the world seemed scary to me, and there was no one to help me in any meaningful sense. My body was changing and I was wondering what it all meant. I was about to enter into uncharted territory, with no guide to provide direction. All this made me vulnerable to whatever came my way. To this day, I feel real empathy for those facing similar realities.

Times of Transition

In time, the fears and questions about life and death would recede. As they did, so did my religious passion and zeal. I fulfilled my yearlong obligation to pray the mourner's *kaddish* prayers for Dad and Grand Pop Salter. After the obligation was fulfilled, I continued to attend the Sons of Jacob services but not nearly as regularly. Gradually the deep practice of my Jewish faith became less and less meaningful.

I do not know how to fully explain the reason for my gradual separation from observant Judaism in general and my involvement with the Sons of Jacob congregation in particular. Clearly, there are limits to the external practice of any religion when it comes to satisfying the needs of the human heart. Gradually, I came to realize that it neither significantly answered my questions nor helped with my struggles. But there were other more important reasons as I look back. I was about to enter high school. Things were changing both in and around me. The friends I had shortly after Dad's passing were finding other friends. I began to feel alone and friendless.

Daily, I would sit at home with Mom and Alice. Weeknights and weekends I would watch TV, listen to the Phillies' games during baseball season, and do little else. It seemed at the time as though Mom was becoming increasingly emotionally fragile. My grandmother would call often to find out how we were doing, but mostly to tell Mom what she should or should not do.

Internally, I found myself with feelings of low self-worth. Some of it was that I was shy and socially awkward; a lot of it had to do with the shame I felt over Dad taking his life. Normal families had a living father and a functioning mother. My family, if you could call it a family, had neither. The more I looked at the normal lives of the people my age, the more I felt abnormal and by extension less valuable. As Mom became what seemed to me less functional, my desire to simply get out from the four walls of the house intensified.

New Neighbors and a Friend

One day, I heard Mom say that a new family moved into a house right behind ours. She soon added that the new family had a boy about my age. Mom was the type to know pretty much everything when it came to the neighbors. While she was drinking one of her seemingly countless cups of instant coffee and looking out a window, she had an excellent view of what was going on. Knowing I needed a friend, she encouraged me to approach the boy and introduce myself. Although I did not have much self-confidence, one afternoon I saw him sitting on his back steps and figured, "What the heck! What did I have to lose?"

Summoning up what courage could be mustered, I nervously and awkwardly approached the boy that I had seen through the window. Rejection is what teenagers typically fear the most and I was no different. Because the pain of rejection could not have been worse than that of loneliness, I made the decision to take the risk.

Bob Simmons and I became best friends from that afternoon on. It turned out that Bob was as lonely as I was, since he was new to the neighborhood. He had just moved to Vineland from Bridgeton, New Jersey, a city about twenty miles away. Bob, his divorced mom Katherine, and his younger sister Donna lived with his grandparents, Tony and Josie Pellicano.

The Simmons and the Pellicanos were nice neighbors, and over time I spent many hours in their house, but it was my friendship with Bob that seemingly came at just the right time. It happened that Bob and I had a lot in common. Although the circumstances were different, Bob and I were both without fathers. His father left his mom when Bob was a young boy and had very little relationship with him. Bob spoke almost nothing about his dad, but it was likely that he felt the same sense of loss as I did.

Perhaps the main thing Bob and I had in common was that we were both desperately in need of friendship. Maybe that was the reason we hit it off as well as we did. It just seemed that we were comfortable hanging out with each other from the very beginning. As I remember, our friendship began sometime during 1966 when I was in the eighth grade, and we remained close until the end of my sophomore year in high school.

While we had a lot in common, Bob and I were also very different in some respects. For one thing, he was a lot more socially confident than I was. This was actually a good thing in that over time, Bob helped me grow in confidence. Another big difference was that Bob was really good when it came to relating to girls. He had a self-assurance about him and I, well to put it mildly, was awkward and terrified of being rejected. If Bob got turned down, it seemed as if it was no big deal. He was back on his feet in no time. However if I got turned down, my confidence was shot. But again, our differences turned out to be a good thing because the more I hung around Bob the more my self-assurance grew in this area. In fact, my first two girlfriends came about as a result of my friendship with him.

Through Bob I made more friends. Johnny Beverly was Bob's closest friend before I came along and although we kind of competed to see who would be his best friend, we became friends in our own right. The three of us along with another friend, John Grassman formed a band and spent a lot of time playing music together. We were not great musicians, especially me, since I played bass very poorly, but it was fun and, like a lot of bands, we dreamed of making it big. Trust me, we had no chance. We did however play at a few dances and parties, which at the very least made us feel good about ourselves.

Bob was a loyal person. Once I was told that the band was encouraged by an unidentified someone that it would do much better with another bass player. A mutual friend mentioned that Bob stood up and said, "If Mike is not part of the band, then I won't be either." That settled the issue because he was the lead singer. While I felt hurt by the attempt to cut me loose, it was great to know that I had such a faithful friend.

My friendship with Bob is another one of those seeming irrelevant details that was actually much more important to my life than I realized at the time. It provided a critical and needed transition for me. Before we became friends, I felt totally overcome by my circumstances. My relationship with Bob enabled me to feel like a normal kid. I started doing things that were fun and my confidence began to increase at least at the margins. Most importantly, I found myself putting my trauma concerning Dad's death in the back of my mind. As time went by, I would be able to force it from my thinking and block out a lot of the pain. That too was a good thing, at least in some respects.

My First Real Job

My friendship with Bob paid dividends in other ways. His grandfather Tony Pellicano worked at Joffe Lumber and Hardware Company. The Joffes who owned Joffe Lumber were no relation to me. Their name is spelled with an *o* while mine is spelled with an *a*. Tony drove an eighteen-wheeler, delivering lumber, windows, and large staircases to construction sites. During the summer of 1968, he told me to put in an application because they needed helpers to unload the trucks when they arrived at the sites. I applied, got the job, and became Tony's helper. He drove and I unloaded. During the long rides to the sites, it was relaxing and almost fun. Sometimes the drives took one to two hours, and I got paid for sitting in the tractor-trailer and talking with Bob's grandfather. I hated the unloading however. Some of the staircases were oak on oak and very heavy, even for two of us.

Working in the summer put some money in my pocket, which was important because Mom had none to spare. I had other small jobs from time to time but nothing of consequence. If I went anywhere in the summer or on Friday nights during school, I needed money to spend. I would try to spend money only when necessary however. Because I was frugal, I was actually able to save money from that first real summer job.

Looking back, the Pellicanos were very nice to me. I'm sure Tony saw my family situation and thought a summer job could help. It was not as though they had much themselves. Tony worked while Josie and Katherine stayed home. On one occasion, Bob's aunt Aggie took the two of us to Wildwood, on the Jersey Shore for a week. We spent the week on the boardwalk trying to pick up girls. Bob was good at it and I was not. Again it was the confidence thing. One night we decided to split up and try our luck on our own. I was so scared, I didn't know where to begin. I simply wandered around and when we rendezvoused a couple of hours later, I lied and boasted of my success. I doubt he believed a word I said.

While this period of my life was relatively brief, it was nonetheless a time in my adolescence that I remember fondly. I enjoyed spending time at Bob's house drinking cans of soda and practicing music. I enjoyed the time I spent with Bob's grandfather Tony while driving to the work sites to unload the lumber. It was nice to have some man figure in my life.

I don't remember much else about my summer working at Joffe Lumber and Hardware. But it does stand out to me for some reason. Maybe it's because there is something really important about a first job. Perhaps it's because I felt worthwhile as a result of working hard for an entire summer. More likely though, it was because it gave me a sense of achievement and some sense of discipline, something I desperately needed—and of course there was that something I seldom had, money.

The Loss of Innocence

One of my vivid memories of this time in my life took place in the fall of 1967. I refer to it as my loss of innocence, not for any sexual reason but rather because it would not be long before I entered another transition. I met an eighteen-year-old named Steve who was well-known in the community for his involvement with drugs. Since I had no real parental supervision, I was a prime candidate for all kinds of experimentation. One day, Steve invited me up to his bedroom where I smoked my first weed. It was only a couple of joints, but it was new and exciting to a fifteen-year-old. Personally, I don't even remember getting that high. Of course, I convinced myself that I was higher than what was really the case. For me, it was all about doing something new, something that other kids my age weren't doing, something I could talk about. It was all about being "cool."

It is important to remember that the fall of '67 was near the beginning of what would turn out to be a cultural upheaval of sorts in the United States. At the time, I did not know anyone else who smoked marijuana or did drugs. I felt as if I was on the ground floor of changing times and really cool as a result.

The afternoon in Steve's bedroom did not mark the beginning of hard-core drug use for me, but it did become the beginning of a new phase of my adolescence. It was a loss of innocence in many respects. Other friends would begin to occupy the majority of my time. These new friends and I would occasionally smoke some marijuana or hashish, but nothing big at least for a while. What that afternoon in Steve's room did mark for me was a sort of transition. It would not be too long before I would choose to engage another search for meaning, one that would involve much of what has come to be known as "The Revolutionary Sixties."

Chapter 8

Phase Two: The Search for Meaning... The Sixties

"There is a time for everything, and a season for every activity
under the heavens: . . .
a time to plant and a time to uproot, . . .
a time to tear down and a time to build, . . .
a time to search and a time to give up, . . .
a time to tear and a time to mend, . . .
a time to love and a time to hate,
a time for war and a time for peace."
—Ecclesiastes 3:1–8

"Let justice roll on like a river,
righteousness like a never-failing stream!"
—Amos 5:24

"Philosophers can debate the meaning of life, but you need a Lord who can declare the meaning of life."
—Max Lucado

A person's growth and development will inevitably intersect with a series of social and cultural events, and these events typically influence that development. In my case, my cultural environment was the turbulent sixties.

Upon reflection, the events of this period of my youth have impacted me significantly and have helped to fashion some core life principles.

Life is filled with numerous twists and turns—some of which end up setting our lives on a different course. My encounter with Steve was one of those significant turning points. The year 1968 was a transitional year for me. As I began to pursue this different course, I began to change both inwardly and in appearance.

For one thing, my awkwardness continued to give way to a greater sense of confidence. Don't get me wrong; I was not an extrovert by any means. Neither should my state be characterized as self-assured. I continued to have complexes that related to who I was. I did not become popular in school or anything like that. Popularity for the most part belonged to teenagers whose parents raised them in healthy environments. Strong families make for self-confidence and self-confidence makes for popularity. At least this is often the case.

I was making progress in this regard however. But there was good news and bad news in the progress I was making. The good news was that I didn't find it hard to make friends. The bad news was I didn't necessarily choose the best kind of friends by most standards. It was here that I also found myself transitioning in my thinking. As time went by, I began to increasingly reject conventional attitudes and norms.

Steve, his brothers Mike and Duane, and their friend Howard were different from anyone else I knew at the time. They were on the cutting edge of the cultural revolution of the sixties. They smoked marijuana and hashish regularly, took other drugs, and played a lot of music. Howard played guitar and played it very well. In time, I would find myself hanging out at Steve's house more and more. Mike and Howard would eventually become my new close friends. Mike and Duane were roughly my age, while Steve and Howard were a couple of years older.

Significant during that time but typically less so today was the fact that all these new friends were African-American. The late 1960s was a time of serious racial divide in America. When a person thinks of the racial tension of the sixties, they most often think of the South. They think of Rosa Parks and her heroic refusal to give up her seat on the bus. They think of Dr. Martin Luther King Jr. and Malcom X. They think of the marches in Selma, Alabama, police dogs attacking blacks who were nonviolently demonstrating for equality, or the racial segregation that was a way of life in that part of the country.

By the end of the sixties however, racial tension had made its way to the northern part of the country as well as the West Coast. A number of the inner cities of the United States were in chaos as racial riots became more common. People who lived in these parts of the country often harbored more sophisticated racial prejudices. I mention this because my hanging out with African-American kids had social consequences. I gradually became part of a new crowd, one that was rejected by many students but sort of admired by others in a weird way.

The subtleties of racism and its sometimes devastating impact on my friends would be among the important influences on my way of thinking during these years. Although I could mention many influences, the one that I remember best was the arrest of my friend Steve for alleged possession of marijuana. I say "alleged" because the rumor among my friends was that the marijuana was planted. Steve was arrested and convicted for the possession of a small amount of marijuana and given what today would be an unthinkable sentence of five years in the state penitentiary.

I certainly cannot state for certain the reason for the harsh sentence nearly fifty years later. I do remember the circumstances that preceded it. Steve was one of the first in our neighborhood to be involved with drugs. He was also one of the first to openly have a white girl as a girlfriend. Even in New Jersey and other places in the northern United States, interracial dating was taboo during the 1960s. Although the precise motivation for the extraordinarily harsh sentence Steve received cannot be known, one thing was undeniable: an eighteen-year-old boy was sentenced to five years in state prison for a crime that did not warrant such punishment.

Whatever his failings, Steve was a very gentle person and did not long survive the effects of his imprisonment. He died a few years later and his mother and brothers were deeply impacted by his tragic fate. Steve's death left a very powerful impression on me as well. I began to first question and then reject institutions of authority. This rejection of authority ultimately would become my excuse to the extent I needed one for using illegal drugs.

Counterculture Politics

My sixties experience can be broken down into two phases. Although one came before the other, there was a time when these phases overlapped. The first largely was an engagement with counterculture politics, while the second was the adoption of a counterculture lifestyle. During both periods I looked the same. I grew my hair long. I had a large salt and pepper Afro, one that was noticed wherever I went.

My interest in politics undoubtedly first came from my family. Politics were a common discussion topic and I remember listening earnestly as my mom's side of the family debated political issues. Mom's side was decidedly liberal in their views as most Jewish people were and still are today. I remember them saying that they voted for Adlai Stevenson for President in both 1952 and 1956, noteworthy because in both cases Dwight D. Eisenhower won these elections by landslides. Similarly, in near unanimous fashion, they declared that they voted for John F. Kennedy in 1960 and Lyndon Johnson in 1964. The one exception on Mom's side was her twin brother, my Uncle Leo, who I remember sheepishly admitting that he voted for Richard Nixon in 1960.

Dad's side of the family however was generally more conservative. I remember Dad stating the reason. Dad worshipped the ground on which Winston Churchill stood. Churchill was a member of the British parliament who later became prime minister. He was a member of the Conservative Party. My father would tell me over and over how Churchill saved Britain from Hitler's tyranny. As a result, Dad's voting patterns were mixed. He voted for the Republican Eisenhower in '52 and '56 but Democrats Kennedy and Johnson in '60 and '64 respectively.

That I can remember my family's political leanings so clearly is an indication of my affinity for politics at so young an age. In 1968, I was only sixteen years old, yet I was politically very aware. The awareness came mostly from my father's early influence. Although all members of my family were interested in politics, Dad was especially so. All of this would practically ensure that when counterculture politics arrived on the scene, I would, at least in the beginning, become extremely interested and involved.

The year 1968 was a tumultuous year in American politics. Two issues dominated the news and produced a near upheaval in the country. The two issues were the continued quest for racial equality on the part of African Americans (the Civil Rights Movement) and the Vietnam War. These two divisive issues were accompanied by two great national tragedies, the assassinations of Dr. Martin Luther King Jr. and Robert F. Kennedy a mere two months apart. While the deaths of these two revered Americans were not directly related, they demonstrated the reality that a country was rapidly becoming torn apart from within.

Politically speaking, 1968 was a perfect storm. The storm's first great event was the decision by President Johnson not to seek a second term. He announced his decision in a speech to the nation on March 31. The second took place just a few days later when Martin Luther King Jr. was assassinated in Memphis, Tennessee, on April 4. King's death was followed by devastating riots in many U.S. cities. On June 5, a third event shook the nation. About two and a half months after entering the race for president, Robert F. Kennedy was shot. He died the next day.

The 1968 Presidential Election

This eventful year was a presidential election year. Entering the 1968 Democratic Convention, two main candidates remained for the nomination, Vice President Hubert H. Humphrey and upstart Senator Eugene McCarthy of Minnesota. McCarthy was the first to challenge Johnson and ran on an anti-Vietnam War plank. It was McCarthy's near win in the New Hampshire Democratic Primary that ultimately caused Lyndon Johnson to decide to not run for a second full term. Humphrey who had the support of the political establishment seemed likely to continue Johnson's policies.

As it turned out, the convention would be remembered more for what took place in the streets of Chicago. A number of groups, some radical and others less so, had planned a gathering to coincide with the Democratic National

Convention which was held in Chicago during the last week of August. News reports stated that over ten thousand demonstrators clogged the streets and were confronted by more than twenty thousand Chicago police officers and National Guard troops. A riot ensued leaving many demonstrators beaten. News reports covered the riot and took much of the attention off of what was taking place inside the Convention Center. Many analysts have concluded that Vice President Hubert Humphrey who ultimately received the nomination never recovered from the disastrous convention.

I remember my sympathies for president were with Senator Eugene McCarthy during that election. Of course, it did not matter much since at the age of sixteen I couldn't vote. I did not dislike Humphrey, but had no real enthusiasm for his candidacy. The person I really disliked was Richard Nixon who would ultimately become President in a very close election. I remember staying up all night at home watching the election returns. I was consumed with the politics of the day because I was passionate about our country's need for social change.

The Civil Rights Movement and the struggle for racial equality would continue throughout the decade and beyond. The same would be true of the antiwar movement, which extended even after the war ended in 1975. While I remained concerned about both of these issues, my political interests would ultimately give way to another, more self-centered phase of my journey.

Drugs and Music

When it came to the culture of the late 1960s, drugs and music often came together. Early in the decade, the main themes of music were either boy meets girl, boy breaks girl's heart, or vice versa. Late in the sixties however, new themes in music began to emerge. These were the varied expressions of the cultural revolution that was taking place in America. New understandings of sexual permissiveness, new attitudes toward civil authority ,as well as the newly found virtues of getting high became increasing prominent in song lyrics.

Rock concerts were nearly always accompanied with the smell of weed and the popping of pills. For many, the experience of listening to or even playing music was enhanced by the effects of a variety of drugs. While all this is still true in many respects today, it all became increasingly popular in the sixties.

Even though I was only in my teenage years, I was increasingly becoming my own master. Mom watched helplessly as her still very young son exposed himself to increasingly dangerous influences. She sensed what was going on, but was helpless to affect it in any appreciable way.

It is easy to see what impact dysfunctional families in general and the lack of a father in particular have on young men. Fathers are meant to provide the pictures of manhood for their sons and, for that matter, their daughters as well. They are meant to both model and speak into the lives of maturing children. I not only lacked a father but an emotionally secure mother as well. As the lack of parental influence intersected the tumult of the 1960s, what happened should have been expected.

Grandma Salter witnessed many of the changes in my life and expressed her increasing concern whenever she saw me. But she did not see me all that much. When she did, she would argue with me, warn me, or try offering rewards for promises of good behavior. Needless to say, nothing anyone said mattered to sixteen-year-old attempting to find his way in life. A father could have or perhaps even would have made a difference, but there was no father. I had to make do without any such influence.

My small, three-bedroom home on 712 Third Street Terrace was merely a place to sleep in those days and on some occasions it was not even that. I came home when I wanted to, slept at friend's houses when I wanted to, and seldom even had the courtesy to let Mom know where I was. I left her to worry about me and worry she did. All of this was of little concern to me. My thoughts were almost exclusively self-directed. All that was on my mind was to find my way.

As I went from my sophomore to my junior year in high school, two patterns began to emerge. I found myself getting high more and more, and I attended school less and less. I managed to pass my junior year but just barely. Somehow I must have been wise enough to not quit school entirely. I certainly could have and Mom could not have done much about it.

Lysergic Acid Diethylamide

As I turned seventeen, my situation went from bad to worse. The main culprit in my decline was my increased drug use. I never sold drugs or even bought drugs for the most part. Neither I nor any in my immediate circle of friends had much money to speak of, or at least that was what we maintained. I actually had some money saved from my job at Joffe Lumber the summer before, but I thought, "Why spend it when I didn't have to." My friends, Howard and Mike, and I acquired the ability to get people to give us the drugs we desired. We did so essentially through manipulation. For whatever reason, teenagers in the Vineland drug culture looked up to us and were often willing to seek our friendship by giving us the drugs we wanted. We would hang out, look cool, and wait for offers. Sometimes they came and sometimes they didn't.

When that failed to work, we had other means. For instance, we had an overweight "friend" who wanted to hang out with us. On multiple occasions, we took advantage of this by talking him into going to a doctor and asking for diet pills to help him lose weight. He came back with a form of Dexedrine, which in the sixties was considered a poor man's speed. It wasn't our favorite drug by any means, but it got us high.

While we liked smoking marijuana, hashish, and doing our poor man's speed, our drug of choice was lysergic acid diethylamide, better known as LSD. In the 1960s, the drug was often called by other names depending on what it was mixed with. LSD is not generally considered to be addictive and as far as Howard, Mike, and I were concerned, it was the perfect way to escape reality for a few hours. We would almost always do the drug together or with other friends because we liked to laugh about how it was influencing our senses.

We also did the drug with others for another reason. One of the potential consequences of LSD was the possibility of a bad trip. I can remember only one occasion that this terrifying experience happened to me personally. These experiences happened enough to others to cause us to always use LSD in community. Because we never really knew precisely what we were taking, every time we dropped acid, we were taking a gamble. Over time the danger caught up with a few of the people we knew. We would hear about it through the grapevine.

Close Calls and Lucky Escapes

When people decide to put their lives at risk, they do so for reasons they don't realize at the time. I believe that these individuals subconsciously believe that life has little meaning and losing it is of little consequence. I am certain that this subconscious belief was a significant part of my risk taking. Don't get me wrong: I did not want to die. In fact, I was afraid of dying. I just didn't see myself with much of a future. Why would I? Nobody close to me had much hope for a good life. Dad obviously hadn't seen a reason to go on living. Mom and Alice were quietly going through their own pain and did not reveal their feelings to me.

I put myself at risk in many ways. Doing drugs could be dangerous. It could lead to overdose, arrest, or accident. It could also lead to being in the wrong places at the wrong times. I recall two occasions in which this was so in my late teen years, although there were numerous others.

Once while I was high, I found myself in a bar with Howard and Mike. The problem was that this bar was a place where African Americans gathered and whites were not welcome. As pointed out earlier, this was a time of extreme racial tension. In our drug-induced states, both my friends and I were oblivious to the dangers of our situation. People gathered around to teach us a lesson, me for being there and my friends for bringing me there. Fortunately for me, an African American high school classmate was there and intervened.

On another occasion, the three of us were in Philadelphia visiting one of Howard's friends. Again, it was a matter of being in the wrong neighborhood and we did not understand the degree of racial animus that was in the inner city. After walking a short distance from our car, I heard threats from a distance. I quickly retreated into the car, locked the doors, and laid down on the seat in genuine fear.

There were other close calls from time to time, but they didn't cause much reconsideration of certain elements of my lifestyle. It was either that I saw myself as impervious to harm or I was just unwilling to acknowledge potential dangers. There were nagging feelings at times that all would not end well for me, but those I would generally ignore.

As I went through my junior year, my life changes were happening quickly, and I had a distinct sense that they were getting a little out of control. Rebellion was becoming a part of my inner fabric, but that was not all. I was also taking risks that a seventeen-year-old might soon regret. No matter, my way was set and there appeared to be no turning back.

Chapter 9
In My Glory at Woodstock

"An Aquarian Exposition: 3 Days of Peace & Music"
—Original billing of the Woodstock Music Festival or Woodstock Music & Art Fair

"Good morning! What we have in mind is breakfast in bed for four hundred thousand."
—Hugh Romney

"This is the way to hear music, I think, surrounded by rolling hills and farmlands, under a big sky."
—Michael Lang, *The Road to Woodstock*

At the beginning of the summer of 1969, I decided to take the money I had in the bank and buy my first car. I had taken the driver's education class during my junior year after receiving my permit. In New Jersey at that time, you had to be seventeen years old to get your driver's license. I had about $850 saved and one day I saw a car in a used car lot that had an $895 sign in its window. It was a brown 1963 Chevy Impala convertible. It was a beauty. I negotiated with the car dealer and he came down to $775. I was able to buy my first car, register it, and have money for a few of tanks of gas to spare. You have to remember that gas in 1969 was as low as 29.9 cents a gallon.

Your first car is usually accompanied by feelings that you have come of age. It is typically a kind of right of passage for a teenager. It sure was for me. I would drive that car down Landis Avenue, Vineland's main drag, see the people I knew, and think I was a big deal. It was also an opportunity to take my friends places. I seemed to have more friends after I got my car, but I don't think I picked up the relationship between the two. It's amazing what a car can temporarily do for a teenager's self-esteem.

Ocean City

I remember spending a lot of time in Ocean City, New Jersey, during that summer. Ocean City was about a forty-minute drive from Vineland and a favorite hangout for students of Vineland High School. Vineland was only thirty miles or so from numerous Atlantic Ocean beaches. It didn't matter whether you were a jock, a greaser, or a druggie, everybody loved Ocean City.

The fact I had a car gave me a real sense of independence. Once a week or so, some friends and I would go to the beach, lie out in the sun, walk the boardwalk, and even do a little drugs if we had them. The Jersey Shore was one of the real benefits of living near the ocean. During the summer of 1969, it was a big part of my existence.

The Atlantic City Pop Festival

From time to time, things would get a little boring. We would get tired of the "same old, same old" and were always looking for something new and exciting. One of us heard of a big event that was going to take place in early August at the nearby Atlantic City Racetrack. The racetrack was only about twenty-five miles from where we lived. The big event came to be known as The Atlantic City Pop Festival. It was one of the first of a series of rock festivals that were common in 1969 and the early 1970s. A couple of friends and I decided to go. To the best of my memory, the tickets were only about fifteen dollars. Some of the biggest bands of the 1960s were on hand and for a bunch of seventeen- and eighteen-year-olds, it was a can't miss event, especially because it was so close.

I have two big memories of The Atlantic City Pop Festival. The first was the near one hundred thousand people who had gathered and the second was the music and drugs. The festival was the first time I could remember people being able to do drugs out in the open with impunity. Going to an event like that provided a lot of opportunities to brag when you got home. I was somebody because I had the ability to do things that a lot of people my age were unable to do. After all they had parents, and parents kept you from doing the things you wanted.

The Main Event

As great as The Atlantic City Pop Festival was to a seventeen-year-old boy seeking an image and an identity, something greater was on the horizon. On the last day of the festival, it was announced that another event was planned. It was to be called the "Woodstock Music and Art Fair" and was to be held somewhere in upstate New York. The two rock festivals were scheduled only a couple of weeks apart and I immediately determined to go to the one in New York. The talk was that it would be much bigger and better.

I did not want to go alone, so I began attempting to enlist potential companions. A lot of my close friends were unable to go, but two seemed excited at the prospect. Because neither attended the Atlantic City Pop Festival, it would be an entirely new experience. My two friends were Bob and Terri. I remember meeting with Terri's father who, after some conversation and expressions of concern, allowed her to go. Bob, for whatever reason, did not seem to have any problem gaining permission.

We set out on a Thursday morning in my 1963 Chevy Impala convertible with great excitement. We had purchased tickets and were ready to have the experience of a lifetime. The drive was about four hours or so through New Jersey and parts of the Pocono and Catskill Mountains. A map guided us to a place called Bethel, New York, near White Lake. We arrived very late on Thursday afternoon, a day before the event was to begin.

Early Surprises

The closer we got to our destination, the more it became apparent that this was going to be a very different experience from the one I had a couple of weeks earlier. About ten miles out, it was common to see people hitchhiking on the road. They were all heading to the same place. When we got to five miles or so from Bethel, traffic came to a near standstill. People were looking for rides rather than walk the last few miles. I picked up two or three, but more asked for "wheels" to get them there. Finally, I let my top down and allowed people to sit on top of the doors, fenders, and anywhere they could find space. What a sight! I would only find out later what it did to the suspension of my Impala. It would never be the same.

When we arrived, we were greeted with another surprise. There were so many people that there were no tickets left for the late arrivers. Additionally, it turned out that the unexpected large number of attendees (estimates later ranged from four to eight hundred thousand people) and their earlier-than-expected arrival would make the original goal of a big, for-profit event unattainable. The crowd pushed down the fence and made it impossible to require tickets or payment. These unanticipated events would ensure that it would be a free concert for many and not a grand moneymaker.

The Venue

What was originally billed as the Woodstock Music and Art Fair was scheduled to be held on an extremely large piece of land at a different location. Organizers, however, met considerable opposition from the townspeople of Walkill, New York, and had to find an alternative site. Eventually, they settled on a location in the town of Bethel. A farmer, Max Yasgur, agreed to allow the event on his very large, nearly six-hundred-acre dairy farm. While many people in the town objected to what some had termed a "hippie music festival," a permit was eventually issued for the visionary event.

The stage was set up at the bottom of a hill. The crowd was able to watch the festival from a hill that looked down on the stage. According to historical accounts, then-Governor Nelson Rockefeller was concerned enough about public safety and the potential of violence that he considered ordering thousands of New York State National Guard troops to the event. He was ultimately dissuaded from doing so. The county did declare a state of emergency and a nearby Air Force base aided in transporting medical supplies. It was reported afterwards, that two people died at Woodstock, one from a drug overdose and one after being run over by a tractor while sleeping in a sleeping bag. It was also documented that two women gave birth during the weekend.

"Freedom"

My memories of the historic rock festival center around a few performers and other unexpected and unanticipated circumstances. Why I remember the things I do and fail to remember other things more than forty-five years later can be relegated to the mysterious aspects of how the human mind works. Generally speaking, like everyone else I was enamored with what was going on. I was a part of something incredibly exciting and for a seventeen-year-old junior in high school that was a thrill beyond thrills.

The first performer, a singer by the name of Richie Havens, set the tone of the weekend event. His performance is best remembered for his long rendition of a song called "Motherless Child." During the song, Richie Havens went into an extended and improvised musical detour called "Freedom." Later it was said that he was asked to keep singing because the acts which were to follow were late in arriving. The improvisation "Freedom" was partially the result of this need to keep performing until other performers were ready.

What made Haven's "Freedom" memorable to many including me was that freedom was something we thought we were achieving. The Woodstock event would, in some ways, be about becoming free. At the time, I believed I was in a sort of heaven. To my way of thinking, it couldn't ever get any better than what I was experiencing. No problems, no responsibilities, no self-esteem issues (or so I thought at the time), life was good. Later, of course, I would come to realize that Woodstock couldn't last forever and heaven was about more than three or four measly days.

Three Days of Peace and Music

The Woodstock Music and Art Fair was alternately billed as "3 Days of Peace and Music." As it turned out, it became a drug-filled music experience. For many of those attending, it was a time to zone out the stuff of life and to just enjoy the escape it provided. Arguments, rules, laws, cops, and everything else that made life miserable were unwelcome. It was intended to be all about peace, love, and, of course, music and drugs.

Among the unwelcome realities of the late 1960s were politics in general and the revolutionary activities of numerous emerging political groups in particular. It was not that no one at the festival had sympathies with these groups. Many in fact did. It was more that protest and the anger that accompanies it did not fit the ambiance of the weekend. Political agitation tends to make people agitated, and that was thought to be destructive to the aura of Woodstock.

One clear example of what I am talking about took place on the second night of the festival, or more accurately early the third morning. While the extremely popular British rock group The Who was performing, a well-known sixties radical, Abbie Hoffman, jumped on stage, took the microphone, and attempted to rant about the jailing of fellow radical John Sinclair. Peter Townshend, lead guitarist of The Who, chased him offstage and reportedly hit him with his instrument in the process. It was rumored that Townshend actually broke the guitar over Hoffman's head, but there is little substantiation for that apparently exaggerated outcome. Many later observed that the guitarist was simply preserving the essence of the Woodstock experience.

Peace, Music and Rain

Perhaps the most memorable event of the Woodstock rock festival was the seemingly never-ending rain. It did not just rain—it poured. Although most attendees will state that it rained the entire event, I do not believe that it did. My memory is that it poured during the second and third days pretty much nonstop.

The rain caused delays during the festival, leaving time between performances. At first, the hundreds of thousands of people were uncomfortable with the idea of getting drenched, but there was nothing to shelter anyone from the torrential downpours. After a while however, everyone reveled in the rain, mud, and discomfort. Even the lack of sanitation was totally ignored. Many people stripped down to their underwear and worse. The elements almost totally removed anyone's inhibitions.

Fortunately, there was a reasonably large pond at one end of Max Yasgur's dairy farm. That pond became a skinny dipper's paradise. After all, lying in the muddy fields for hours left everyone filthy. The pond became a virtual bathhouse, at least until everyone heard that the music was going to resume.

The Grand Finale

The Woodstock rock festival turned out to be a gathering of some of the biggest names when it came to the counterculture music of the late sixties. Bands and vocalists such as The Who; Jefferson Airplane; The Grateful Dead; Janis Joplin; Credence Clearwater Revival; Crosby, Stills, Nash & Young; The Band; Santana; Blood, Sweat & Tears; Arlo Guthrie; Richie Havens; and Joan Baez were only a representation of the more than thirty performers. Like everyone else, I had my favorites. I happened to love The Band, Creedence Clearwater Revival, and Crosby, Stills, Nash & Young.

For virtually everyone however, at least for those who stayed to the end, the greatest musical memory was the performance of Jimi Hendrix. His rendition of "The Star Spangled Banner" while wearing his red headscarf and blue fringe jacket formed perhaps the sixties' most memorable musical episode. Pictures of it abound and it remains one of the great iconic moments in sixties lore.

Jimi Hendrix was the last of the Woodstock musicians to perform. For those like me who arrived late Thursday afternoon, it was a five-day experience rather than three. Because of the delays caused by the rain, it was sometime mid-Monday morning that Hendrix took the stage. As I recall, it was almost noon before he was finished. Since my two friends and I stayed until the event was completely over, we were able to navigate our way through the significantly reduced crowd to right near the stage. We had front row seats for one of the iconic moments of the 1960s and, believe me, we told everyone who would listen about it.

The Aftermath

For most of my ilk, Woodstock was the pinnacle of the decade. For whatever reason, it was all downhill from there. Woodstock has been relived time and again. It has been made into a movie and numerous documentaries. There was even a forty-year reunion for participants to revel in the memories (for the record, I did not attend the reunion).

However, it would not be long before life would change for many who attended the signature event of 1960s counterculture. This was true for even some of the performers. Within two years or so from the conclusion of The Woodstock Music and Art Fair, two of its most noteworthy musicians, Jimi Hendrix and Janis Joplin, died of alleged drug overdoses. One could only guess about the number of the half million or so attendees who experienced the same fate.

The truth is "3 Days of Peace and Music" is one thing and a life of peace and music is quite another. As far as I was concerned, the euphoria of Woodstock would never be repeated. I returned home with Terri and Bob, and came back to the mundane and the day-to-day monotony. When I came home, I returned to bored friends, a worried mother, sister, and grandmother, my senior year of high school, and my seemingly meaningless and lonely existence. As August 1969 turned into September, I began to realize that Woodstock was over, and life would go on as uncertain as it was.

Chapter 10
The Passing of Hope and a Desperate Night

"What is crooked cannot be straightened;
what is lacking cannot be counted"
—Ecclesiastes 1:15

"Would you tell me, please,
which way I ought to go from here?"
"That depends a good deal on where you want to get to."
"I don't much care where—"
Then it doesn't matter which way you go."
—Adapted from a conversation between Alice and the Cheshire Cat in Lewis Carroll's *Alice in Wonderland*

The fall of 1969 and the spring of 1970 were in many ways about leftover memories. It seemed the more I tried to relive the glory of the Woodstock experience, the emptier it felt. I would talk incessantly to people I hung out with and they would simply smile and say "wow," or "cool," or something else meaningless. Even Howard and Mike, the two guys I hung out with the most would simply smile or nod. I found out that people didn't care much about my experiences. They were caught up in their own stuff.

People are pretty much the same. They love to talk about their exciting experiences to anyone who will listen and give token acknowledgements to the exploits of others. People were just like me. They sought to establish their own "cool credentials" in order to compare favorably with anyone within their immediate environment.

It was becoming clear to me that attending the great Woodstock event was less and less significant in the overall scheme of things in my life. The inescapable routine of mundane living was taking over. My senior year was about to begin and my prospects afterward seemed very minimal. Excitement was rapidly giving way to uncertainty. It was also obvious to me that although graduating high school was a big deal to a lot of people, my graduation was going to be a virtual non-event.

Senior Year and Graduation

Graduation, in fact, would by no means be a guarantee. As I progressed through the twelfth grade, I began to spiral downward. The spiral was slow but consistent and progressive. Things just seemed to continually go wrong. To start with, my '63 Impala convertible gave way after about a year and a half of use, midway through my senior year. It was not the car's fault. It had experienced significant adversity in the short period of time it was in my possession. First, the weekend at Woodstock took a toll. I believe up to ten people rode on the hood, trunk and bumpers for a number of miles as we made our way to Max Yasgur's dairy farm. Early in the fall, the car was stolen while a couple of friends of mine and I were spending the day in Philadelphia. The car was recovered but in a damaged state. Finally, it succumbed to an overall lack of care. You see, its owner had no clue of how to take care of a motor vehicle.

Unfortunately, there was no money to replace it, so I was back to walking everywhere I had to go. I hated taking the bus to school, but because Vineland High School was about three miles from my home, it was necessary. During the last half of my senior year, I began missing school repeatedly. All told I missed close to eighty days of school. Looking back, I honestly do not know how I passed. I sometimes think people in the administration wanted to get rid of me because I had a reputation as a "druggie" and overall bad influence. My grades were a mix of Cs, Ds and Fs, but I eventually made it to graduation.

I ended up graduating near the bottom of my graduating class of about six hundred students. Two things stick out in my memory when it came to my graduation ceremony. I remember people laughing when I received my diploma because my hair was a very long, bushy Afro and it stuck out from my graduation cap. I also remember no celebration whatsoever on the part of my immediate family. For others, it was a time of celebrating a doorway to the future by friends and family, but not for me. No one made a big deal of it.

It had been a little more than five years since my father had taken his life. My situation could have easily been predicted. God's plan is for young boys to grow up in healthy families. His intent is for them to have fathers and healthy mothers. When they do not, they are at risk. Healthy families are anchors for young boys during their teenage years and where there are no anchors they will drift—and I was drifting with little or no idea where I would land.

There were times when I would think about Dad. I would wonder why he felt so empty and viewed life as so hopeless. In my most despairing moments, I would wonder what he was thinking as he suffocated himself. When I felt the worst,

I would go to where my friends hung out and hope they had some drugs, preferably LSD, to spare. Getting high was my answer and escape.

Trying to Relive the High

I did have one other plan during the summer of 1970. It was to try to relive the summer of 1969 and find another Woodstock. Other rock festivals were scheduled during July and August of 1970, and I was determined to experience another "three days of peace and music." The lack of a car would have been enough to discourage the attempt for some, but I was determined to go searching for another unforgettable experience or two. This time I could not find anyone interested or available to go with me, so I decided to go alone and hitchhike my way to bliss.

The Powder Ridge Rock Festival was scheduled near Middletown, Connecticut, July 31 through August 2 of that summer, and I set out about three days before the event on my two feet with a backpack and thumb in the air. I found places on the side of the road to sleep and ate whatever food I had packed, mostly of the canned variety. People would pick me up and take me various distances at times sharing food supplies. I arrived a couple of days ahead of the event only to find that a judge had issued a court order canceling the rock festival. I was not alone in my disappointment. Some thirty thousand people had gathered for the Woodstock encore and were in the same situation I was, although most of them had transportation. We did spend a part of the weekend listening to a few local bands and getting high, so all was not lost. I returned home a couple of days later.

Undaunted, I heard of another rock festival that was to take place the next week. This one would be a bit more of a challenge since it was to take place in Ontario, Canada. With little money in my pocket, my backpack filled with more canned food, and my thumb in the air, I began the journey to the Strawberry Fields Festival being held at the Mosport Park Raceway about sixty-five miles east of Toronto. My journey was an exciting one. I met lots of people who shared their food and, on one occasion, even a place to stay for a night. There was a problem though. Canadian border police were turning people back who did not have enough money to justify their stay. I was fortunate that the people who picked me up as I was hitchhiking just before crossing the Buffalo Peace Bridge between Buffalo, New York, and Ontario, temporarily gave me the minimum requirement to get into the country providing I gave it back when we crossed into Canada.

The three days of music at Strawberry Fields were remarkably unmemorable. Maybe it was because the number of big-name musicians was much fewer or perhaps it was because there was only one Woodstock. I can't say. It just wasn't the same. I returned home somewhere in the middle of August feeling a little unfulfilled and disappointed. My attempt to revisit the euphoria of the year before fell flat.

Jesus Freaks and the Gospel

After arriving home, I did what I always did—I returned to the place my crowd of friends hung out. It was a concrete wall next to an abandoned movie theatre on East Landis Avenue in Vineland. We called it "The Wall," an appropriate title since that was exactly what it was. It was a leftover concrete block façade that remained after some building was torn down. The Wall was the place we gathered to meet friends, exchange money for drugs, or in my case hope someone would give me some. Typically, I would hang out there with

Howard, Mike, and a few assorted wayward types.

One Friday night during August, there was the arrival of a new element at our hangout, one that wasn't entirely welcome. An individual named Bob, his brother Steve, and a younger guy by the name of John Wilhelm would come by to bring us what they called "good news." Bob was the leader. He had long blonde hair and a constant but somewhat sickening smile on his face that never left. Bob and his brother Steve, who was less pushy and much more likable, were well-known and well-regarded guitarists, and John was a drummer. A couple of weeks before they had "encountered Jesus Christ" (so they said anyway) while at the Ocean City, New Jersey, boardwalk and made it their mission to tell everyone whether they wanted to hear it or not. I can still remember Bob's opening line every time he saw us. "How are you doing?" he would ask. When you responded "All right," he would retort, "You could be doing better!" After a while we figured out that our best defense against Bob was to not make eye contact.

We began calling Bob, Steve, and John "Jesus freaks." Before I go on, perhaps it would be worthwhile to give some background to the term, since it would become common to the Jesus Movement era of the 1970s. One term for those in the sixties counterculture was "hippie." Another, not-so-well-known term was "freak," because in a lot of peoples' minds that's what they looked like. Someone who looked like a "hippie" or "freak" but talked about Jesus all the time was given the name "Jesus freak."

Commonly, when the three would come by, most of us would walk away and act like we had important transactions to make. Invariably, we would try to get away when cornered by them, but that often proved easier said than done. If we couldn't get away, we were subjected to "the gospel" until we could find a way out of the conversation. Bob's persistence would usually make that very difficult. Looking back, although our body language would make our feelings unmistakably clear, he was remarkably unaffected by our rejection and amazingly resilient.

Before I go on, I want to say one more thing about Bob's gospel. I would realize later that it was absolutely uncompromising and thoroughly biblical. Bob and his fellow believers would never mince words. His message was long on our spiritual need and short on false promises. He would talk about sin and, although it would bother me, it would stick in my mind.

On occasion during my long walks home, my thoughts would return to five years earlier when I was returning home after praying mourner's kaddish for my father. I would think about the questions: Who is God?, Would I go to heaven if I died?, and How could I know for sure? It occurred to me that for the first time someone was giving me an answer to the second question. Maybe it wasn't the right answer, from my point of view, but it was an answer. According to Bob, Steve, and John, the answer was no, I would not go to heaven.

The Walls Close In

Unfortunately, for the most part, the gospel initially became little more than an irritant to my thinking. My answer was more drugs as long as Howard, Mike, and I could continue to get people to give them to us for free. Sometimes it worked and sometimes it didn't. In all, by the end of the summer, I was totally directionless and simply floating around from day to day. I would hang out with friends if they were around, otherwise each day became more boring, lonely, and utterly self-centered.

One afternoon, I sat on a street curb in front of what I remember to be a funeral home and just closed my eyes with my head down, resting on my folded arms. I may have dosed off for a brief moment. I heard a noise around me and looked up to find a policeman walking toward me. Parked in the road nearby was his police car with lights flashing. Since my friends and I were known by the local police, I was not totally surprised at what followed. He told me to stand up against his patrol car and proceeded to search me. Fortunately for me, I always made it a practice never to carry drugs on my person. I had too many friends who were caught with drugs in their possession and ended up in jail. The system at that time was pretty harsh on drug offenders because community leaders were trying to purge it from the community. They viewed it as a real crisis. Actually, not carrying drugs was pretty easy for me since I was just a user and seldom had more on me than I could use at a given moment.

Although the policeman found nothing, he wasn't through. He decided to take me to the station and keep me there for a few hours without charging me. When I asked why and what I had done, the policeman's supervisor, a lieutenant, simply stated that I was under suspicion for drug activity. I remember being left in a room with just a table and uncomfortable chair for hours waiting for someone to come in and let me go. Finally, early that evening the original officer came in and told me I was being released. He put me in his police vehicle and drove me home.

The sight of the police car pulling up in front of the house put Mom into a state of panic. She went from screaming at me to pleading with me. Part of it, I'm sure was the embarrassment of a police car dropping her son off at her house for everyone to see. But it was clearly much more than that. Mom was deeply concerned about my welfare and completely helpless to alter my situation. After that event, Mom seemed to become more and more agitated about my life prospects. One evening, I left the house and she followed me. About a block from the house, I saw her, turned around, and asked her what she was doing. She started to cry and pleaded with me to come home. When I refused, she laid down in the middle of the street and said that she would not get up until I came home. Not knowing what to do, I went home with her promising to never do drugs again. It was a lie, of course. I had no intention of following through on the promise. I simply wanted to get her off the street and back to the house.

Although dysfunctional in some ways, Mom instinctively knew that I was spiraling down and feared how it would end. Undoubtedly, the fact that Dad had taken his life increased her anxiety. She knew that the walls were closing in around me in ways I couldn't perceive. My life was becoming listless and my state of mind was starting to border on depression. I didn't know what I was going to do from one day to the next.

The walls were closing in on me in other ways, too. One day I met John Wilhelm near "The Wall" and he invited me to listen to his band to play music at their house. John, Steve, and a couple of other musicians including my friend Howard were planning a jam session, and a lot of my friends were going to be there. John and Steve, although newly minted Jesus Freaks, were well liked by people I knew and got along well with everybody. By contrast, few of us viewed Bob that way. As I mentioned, Bob was real pushy about Jesus and typically alienated the people he was attempting to influence.

I recall that during a break John talked with a girl named Sue Griffith and me about Jesus. Sue was a close friend of mine. I really admired Sue for a number of reasons. She was caring and genuine. Sue and John were probably the most genuine people I knew. Somehow when John spoke, I was willing to listen and listen I did.

John shared the gospel humbly, sincerely, and without compromise. He stated that we were all sinners and needed Jesus' death on the cross to make us right in God's sight. During the conversation, I remember asking John what God would do with Jewish people who did not believe in Jesus. Would they go to hell simply because they did not believe in Jesus? That, of course, was the logical question for me to ask since I was a Jew. He replied that people would not go to hell because they were Jewish. Individuals would go to hell because they were sinners and, because of their sin, they could not have a relationship with a holy God. This was true whether a person was a Jew or a Gentile. While I was offended by John's answer, I was not offended by John. His eyes radiated a gentle, sincere demeanor, and for whatever the reason, I found myself appreciating his honest attempt to answer my question.

My question and John's answer would become important as I would find myself on occasions remembering his words. I was unconvinced on two points however. First, I did not consider myself to be too bad to merit God's acceptance. I thought I was good, especially when comparing myself to others. Second, the notion that a Jew does not believe that Jesus is God was deeply ingrained within me. I never forgot the shema that I would recite on numerous occasions in the prayer services at the Sons of Jacob synagogue I attended as a boy and young teenager. "Hear, O Israel; The LORD our God, the LORD is One (Deuteronomy 6:4).

As summer gave way to fall, I enrolled in Cumberland County College, a local community college. I chose political science as my major since nothing else interested me in the least. The experience was meaningless mostly because I was too undisciplined to attend classes regularly. I also had to hitchhike to even get there. I moved out from my home to join a few other friends who had taken up residence in a makeshift barn with a series of lofts that had mattresses for sleeping. It was closer to the college and I could walk there if I was unable to get a ride hitchhiking. It was bare survival. I had no car, no money, no ambition, and little food for the most part.

One Desperate Night

The more aimless I grew, the more I felt that walls were closing in on me. I sensed what Mom instinctively knew. I could not keep going the way I was going. Early in October 1970, things began to change rapidly. In retrospect, I can see the clear working of God. I can now recognize that His hand was heavily engaged in my life circumstances not only in this brief period, but in and through all the events of my life.

It was the night of October ninth that would ultimately prove to be a turning point. It began innocently enough. I went to "The Wall" to hang out as usual. I was expecting to meet a few friends, but those friends didn't show. Other people did approach me to go and party with them and for whatever reason, I didn't want their company. They had given me drugs in the past and I didn't have an excuse so I made up some story to explain why I couldn't go. It was a lie but on that night I was totally okay with anything that could get me out of the situation. I don't know why, but my willingness to do anything to further my desired ends bothered me that night. Lying to people who had given me free drugs troubled my conscience. It occurred to me that I was okay with using people when I needed them, but I felt that night they were unworthy of my company. I, for the first time, saw myself as a hypocrite and for good reason—I was a hypocrite.

It is amazing to me that the Holy Spirit uses seemingly small things like this to get our attention when the time is right. I remembered John's words about all of us being sinners and somehow I made a connection. I tried to pass off the connection and I did for a while, but it would return.

One other thing happened that night that startled me. One of the friends that I was supposed to meet was Sue Griffith. Later, I heard an amazing thing. After asking someone if they had seen Sue, Howard, Mike, and another friend, the person told me that Sue had become a Jesus freak. I was stunned and refused to believe that it was true.

It was about ten or eleven o'clock when I came across an acquaintance who was giving away some LSD. From time to time, people would come by giving samples away to stir up future business. Howard, Mike, and I depended on this as one way to secure the drugs we wanted to use. I gladly accepted it and promised I would tell him how the "trip" went during the next day or two. I took it and hitchhiked to the barn where I was staying, fully expecting to see some other friends when I arrived. It was seldom quiet there because people always came and went.

"Always" however did not include the night of October 9, 1970. I arrived shortly before midnight only to find the place empty. I waited expecting people to arrive but no one did. But that would be the least of my problems. The acid I took was laced with something and that became evident as the minutes went by. I became agitated and began to hallucinate, seeing things that terrified me. I was alone with no one to talk me down. All I could do was try to walk around the barn and hope it would pass. It didn't. I went upstairs to the loft I slept in and found my radio. My greatest need at the time I thought was to hear music or at least some sound to drown out the voices in my head. My radio was always turned to WMMR, a Philadelphia rock station. Maybe some familiar music would be able to calm me. It didn't. As hour after hour went by, everything got worse. I screamed but there was no one there to hear. It got so bad that I entertained the notion of killing myself, not that I wanted to, but I just wanted the trip to end and it wouldn't. For a moment, I really thought that night would be my last on earth. I was terrified and felt all alone.

In my most terrifying moments, strange things began to happen. It seemed as if songs about Jesus and God were featured that night on WMMR. I doubt they were featured, it just seemed to me as if they were. Songs about Jesus and God were not uncommon in the late sixties and early seventies. I remember two playing during my most panic driven moments during that evening. They were "Jesus Is Just Alright" by the Byrds and "Spirit in the Sky" by Norman Greenbaum.

Some of Greenbaum's words were especially poignant and stuck in my mind. In the song he implied that he was going to heaven when he died, but that he needed Jesus' help. He proclaimed "Prepare yourself it's a must, Gotta have a friend in Jesus." So when you die, He could recommend you to that "spirit in the sky."

I'm not sure I connected with the theology (to the degree there was a theology) of the songs, but the songs had a significant calming effect on me. I remember waking up about ten the next morning, still alone but alive and at least in possession of my faculties. The songs faded into the back of my mind, and I hitchhiked my way back to town to "The Wall." I was looking for friends, but they weren't to be found that morning either. So what? I thought. What could they do for me anyway? It didn't seem as if there were answers anymore.

The Many Faces of Being Lost

I felt tired in every way. I was physically, mentally, and emotionally tired. That reality weighed heavily on me as I sat on the same street curb where I had sat when I was picked up by the police officer a few months prior. Apprehensive thoughts went through my mind during those moments. Instead of "What would I do with my life?," I wondered "How will my life end?" Would it end like Dad's had ended? Would I die of a drug overdose? Perhaps I would just jump off of a ledge after another bad trip. That's one face of being lost.

Maybe I wouldn't die prematurely. There was the jail or prison option. Some of my friends took that route. What would I do in prison? What was it like? What happens when you get out? Steve, Mike's brother, died after getting out of prison. Living with no future is another face of being lost.

What about living without a job, an education, or a career? My best case scenario might be that. Sitting around doing essentially nothing was a possible destiny. Was this the way Dad was thinking as he stood in that field and placed a bag over his head, if that was indeed the way his life had ended? Hopelessness is yet another face of being lost.

And then there was one more—what if what John had said was true? My lies and selfishness seemed to overwhelm my protests of alleged goodness. I remembered my hypocrisy the night before. I thought about how I used my overweight friend to get Dexedrine so I could get high. What about how I treated my hurting and overwhelmed mother? I was really feeling like an unworthy sinner who was truly separated from God.

Lost was the best way to describe me. It is the best way to describe the state of all humans who are alienated from their Creator. It covers everything. It describes our loneliness, our hopelessness, our fatigue about life, and most of all our separation from the One who created us. It implies we are drifting and unable to find our way. As I sat on that curb around one in the afternoon on Saturday, October 10, 1970, one thing was certain to me: I was lost, utterly and completely lost.

Part 2:

What It Means to Be Found

Part 2

Introduction to Part 2

Amazing grace how sweet the sound
That saved a wretch like me.
I once was lost but now am found
Was blind but now I see.
—"Amazing Grace" John Newton (my emphasis)

"Suppose one of you has a hundred sheep and loses one of them. Doesn't he leave the ninety-nine in the open country and go after the lost sheep until he finds it? And when he finds it, he joyfully puts it on his shoulders and goes home. Then he calls his friends and neighbors together and says, 'Rejoice with me; I have found my lost sheep.'"
—Luke 15:4–6

"But while he was still a long way off, his father saw him and was filed with compassion for him; he ran to his son, threw his arms around him and kissed him. The son said to him, 'Father, I have sinned against heaven and against you. I am no longer worthy to be called your son.' But the father said to his servants, 'Quick! Bring the best robe and put it on him. Put a ring on his finger and sandals on his feet. Bring the fattened calf and kill it. Let's have a feast and celebrate. For this son of mine was dead and is alive again; he was lost and is found.'"
—Luke 15:20–24

While the effects of harm can accumulate over long periods of time, a rescue can take place in a breath. Fortunately for Theoden, king of Rohan, his rescue was at hand. Although his situation was hopeless and he had no strength to withstand the wicked wizard Saruman, another wizard, Gandalf, knew of his devastating plight and was determined to set him free. And set him free, he did. The havoc that resulted from the king's bondage was months in the making, but his deliverance took only moments. The liberated King Theoden gradually regained his strength and determination, and summoned resources that he had no idea were available.

Once released from his bondage, the trajectory of Thoeden's life changed entirely. He became a dramatically transformed individual who was then free to achieve his intended destiny. Courageously, he led his people in battle and honored his forefathers through his bravery.

People who are set free by Jesus experience similar realities. There are a number of points of comparison to the deliverance of Theoden in the *The Lord of the Rings*. For one, people have no power to save themselves. Secondly, they are delivered by a power greater than that which had enslaved them. Finally, they do not pursue the one who liberates, the liberator pursues them.

The New Testament expression *found* has great significance. To start with, the New Testament never speaks of it in terms of us finding God. We are not the ones doing the searching. He is not hiding from us, eluding all of our desperate attempts to locate Him. To the contrary, God is not even on our radar when we struggle to navigate our way through life. True, we are looking for answers, but we are looking in all the wrong places.

It is essential to note in the Parable of the Lost Sheep that it is not the lost sheep that is searching for the shepherd. It is the other way around. The shepherd diligently searches for the sheep that is lost. He does so to the point of leaving the ninety-nine who are already in his possession. The shepherd never gives up the search. He searches until he finds the one that had been lost. When the shepherd finds the missing sheep, he puts it on his shoulders, goes home, and calls his friends and neighbors together to celebrate. The lost sheep, by contrast, was utterly helpless not knowing its way back.

The truth is God finds us. He is the one who seeks and saves those who are lost (Luke 19:10). The initiative is all God's. He continually woos us and calls us back to Himself. God never rests until we are found.

When we are found by the Lord, all kinds of wonderful things begin in us. They are not immediate, neither are they automatic. By that I mean they take time and cooperation on our part. But they do begin and continue because God finds us in order to fulfill His ultimate, eternal purpose—to form us into subjects of His great Kingdom.

Just as being lost implies a state of confusion and disorientation, being found implies a state of restoration and completeness. God not only begins the work but He continues it to completion (Philippians 1:6). He heals the brokenness of our hearts, transforms us through the renewal of our minds, and makes us into people who can lead others into the same miraculous journeys.

All this happens in the most mysterious and mystical way. God's miracle in us takes place through good times and bad, through periods of joy and sorrow, and through victory and defeat. The same God who took the initiative to find us, takes the initiative to complete us. In everything we can have the utmost assurance that He works all things for the good of those who love Him and are called according to His purpose (Romans 8:28).

It is with this in mind that I turn to the second part of my story. It will contain a set of events that are different from many who have gone through faith journeys. But it is also true that it has left me in the same state that characterizes countless millions of others as well. I have in every sense—been found.

Chapter 11
The First Day of the Rest of My Life

"The Spirit of the Sovereign Lord is on me, because the Lord has anointed me to proclaim good news to the poor. He has sent me to bind up the brokenhearted, to proclaim freedom for the captives and release from darkness for the prisoners, to proclaim the year of the Lord's favor and the day of vengeance of our God, to comfort all who mourn, and provide for those who grieve in Zion—to bestow on them a crown of beauty instead of ashes, the oil of joy instead of mourning, and a garment of praise instead of a spirit of despair. They will be called oaks of righteousness, a planting of the Lord for the display of his splendor."
—Isaiah 61:1–3

"Therefore, if anyone is in Christ, the new creation has come: The old has gone, the new is here!"
—2 Corinthians 5:17

"When people stop believing in God, they don't believe in nothing—they believe in anything."
—G.K. Chesterton

The Messiah, God's Anointed One, came to earth with a mission. That mission was declared hundreds of years prior to His arrival on this planet by the prophet Isaiah. The prophet promised this Gift to the human race would bind up wounds, bring freedom, comfort those who are deeply sad, and replace ashes and despair with beauty and praise. On the tenth of October 1970, that ancient promise began to be fulfilled in my life. I say *began* because I cannot say for certain exactly when I came to saving faith. In fact, I tend to think that it was more a process than a moment in time. There may have been a precise moment in time when my heart was regenerated and I was justified, made righteous in God's sight. There may have been a moment in time when I was forgiven of my sins and reconciled to the Father. I just can't say precisely when that was. I know when the process began and I will leave the rest to the realm of mystery.

A Watershed Encounter

My physical situation was virtually identical to the time I sat on the curb some weeks earlier. My eyes were closed and my head rested on my folded arms. I vaguely remember wondering if I would be picked up again and taken to the police station. At that point, I don't think it mattered. I wasn't carrying. As usual, there were no drugs on my person. What was far more important to me was my state of life. It wasn't good and stood no chance of getting better.

As before, I heard a noise of someone approaching and lifted my head up. This time it was not a policeman; it was Sue Griffith. God could not have made a more perfect choice as to the person who would enable me to take the first step in what would turn out to be a watershed encounter. As I stated previously, Sue and John Wilhelm were the two people I trusted most.

My first thought was, "Was it true? Had Sue become one of those 'Jesus freaks'?" She looked at me, smiled, and asked if I was okay. Of course I was not. I was anything but okay. I was empty, guilty, confused, and completely lost in every biblical sense of the term.

Sue proceeded to tell me what I instinctively knew. She had "given her life to Jesus." While I did not know exactly what that meant, I did know that for her it was a big deal—a big, life-changing deal. She quietly asked me if I was ready to have my life experience a change. I felt numb from the night before. I also felt the absence of any of the barriers that up to then had been in the way. No longer was I convinced of my goodness. Any sense of betrayal to my Jewish heritage should I believe in Jesus seemed inconsequential and unimportant when compared to my current mental state. Sue apparently did not feel adequate to explain my spiritual need further, so she asked if I would be willing to talk to Bob, the leader of this fledgling band of Jesus freaks who happened to live a couple of short blocks from where I was sitting. I offered no resistance.

I barely recall the short walk to Bob's house. I just remember him meeting Sue and me at the door and leading me to his upstairs bedroom. Bob lived with his mother and stepfather who was a detective in the Vineland Police Department, although not the one I had previously encountered. Bob shared the gospel with me. It was very similar to the message John Wilhelm had shared with me some weeks earlier. Because Bob had such a strong personality, I found his persuasive arguments difficult to resist, especially in my confused state. He seemed so sure about everything and I felt sure of nothing. When he asked me if I wanted to repeat a prayer, I again found it difficult to resist. I prayed with him somewhere around 1:30 in the afternoon of October 10, 1970.

I looked up at Bob and he pointed me to the poster on his wall. It read,

"Today is the first day of the rest of your life."

My first response was to greet Bob's smile with one of my own. He told me that I was a follower of Jesus now. He was much more convinced of this reality than I was however. In my non-resisting mode, I simply agreed even though I was in all truthfulness full of doubts. I doubted that I could or even wanted to follow Jesus. I doubted what saying a simple prayer really meant in the scheme of things. I doubted what I would be doing or believing tomorrow or the next day. At that moment, for some reason it did not matter. Bob was happy, Sue was happy, and I was . . . at least for the moment.

A Pinch of Leaven

On one occasion, Jesus told his disciples a parable. He declared, "The kingdom of heaven is like yeast that a woman took and mixed into about sixty pounds of flour until it worked all through the dough" (Matthew 13:33).

In the parable, Jesus was referring to the transforming power of God's kingdom when it enters both a person's life and the world at large. Once it enters a residence, it begins to conquer all resistance. When a person truly believes in the work of Christ and commits to His Lordship, the Spirit of God takes up residence in that person's heart. At that moment the transforming power is unleashed. Little by little, the Holy Spirit increases His dominion until the person's entire life is changed.

I cannot say when that power was unleashed in me. Theologically, I have my doubts as to whether or not it was that moment I repeated Bob's prayer and looked up and saw that poster. As I said, I remember being not entirely convinced of my commitment. My heart was not fully ready at that moment. I do know however that the prayer and the poster on the wall represented a signature moment of something.

Shortly, after praying the sinner's prayer with Bob, he challenged me to do something radical, which was totally consistent with his strong personality. Bob challenged me to accompany Sue and him to "The Wall" and tell all who were there that I had given my life to Jesus Christ. Again I succumbed to Bob's insistence. How could I not? Bob quoted the words of Jesus to me that declared, "Whoever acknowledges me before others, I will also acknowledge before my Father in heaven. But whoever disowns me before others, I will disown before my Father in heaven" (Matthew 10:32).

I certainly did not want to be disowned by Jesus. So being afraid of that possibility and a little in awe of the moment, I did what Bob asked. All the while however, I sincerely doubted that my life would be changed in any permanent way or that I had crossed a line that would last my entire life. After I fulfilled Bob's request, I committed to meet Bob, Sue, and John the next day and walked back to my house, about a mile and a half away.

As I headed toward home late that afternoon, I resolved to not do a few things. I determined to not get carried away with this "Jesus thing." Don't get me wrong. There was something compelling about Bob, Bob's brother Steve, and especially John and Sue. There was something about their certainty, faith, and deep sense of serenity. Apart from the people I just told who were at "The Wall," I determined to keep this essentially to myself. Particularly, there would be no mentioning this to Mom or Alice. I would wait until I was more certain before I would do something that would cause a reaction for which I was not then prepared.

The Leaven Spreads

For the next few days, I met with Bob, John, and Sue regularly. We would pray together and mostly allow Bob to preach at us. I don't want to sound as though I was negative when it came to Bob, but it was just that his personality was overbearing and at times grated on me. John and Sue didn't seem to have a problem with him for the most part, but I did.

As much as I resisted Bob's dominating personality, he was very important to what would turn out to be a divine work in my life. Left to myself, I would have been content to place Jesus in my hip pocket and go on living my life on my own terms. I wanted the benefits of potentially having Jesus in my life but was content with giving Him minimal control over the way I lived. Bob would have none of that however. He would continually quote passages of Scripture that emphasized that Jesus required our complete submission to His Lordship. Gradually even though I found myself wanting to resist Bob's controlling ways, I was becoming increasingly influenced by what he had to say. I guess I instinctively understood the truth of what he was saying.

It was on a Friday afternoon six days after my initial encounter with Jesus that I ran into Bob and John in town. Bob told me about an all-night prayer meeting that he had heard was taking place at a church about two miles from my house. He said that the two of them were planning on going and asked if I wanted to go as well. My first response was to think how could people pray all night. As usual however Bob's persistence prevailed and I found myself walking with the two of them into the foyer of Chestnut Assembly of God at about nine o'clock or so that night. In the sanctuary, the pews were virtually empty, but in the front there were about a half a dozen people praying in a way that seemed very strange to me.

A woman was sitting in a chair in front of the altar area. She was surrounded by four men. They had their hands on her head and were praying in a very loud manner. There was one other woman there, a friend of the woman being prayed for who was watching. Keep in mind the only times I had set foot in a church building were during those occasions when my friend George Booskos and his family took me to Philadelphia Eagles football games and we had to attend the Greek Orthodox Church beforehand. I had thought that this church would be similar, but was I mistaken. Instead of quiet periods of kneeling and standing, the three of us sat in the back and watched the show. Four men were yelling at the top of their lungs and a poor woman was sitting on a chair with their hands on her head. "What in the world has she done?" I thought as I watched intently.

Fortunately, Bob knew what was going on. In retrospect, I am amazed that he knew so much about these kinds of things considering he had only been a follower of Jesus for a couple of months. But he did know a lot, at least compared to John and especially me. Bob told me that the woman hadn't done anything wrong, but they were praying for her to receive the baptism in the Holy Spirit. I asked Bob what that was and he knew because he said he had received the very same thing. He asked John and me if we wanted to "receive the Baptism." Again it's important to understand when Bob asked a question like that, we always knew the answer he expected to receive.

The men prayed over the woman for what seemed to be quite a while with no results. After she left the chair to sit on the front pew, Bob nudged John and me to go forward and we did very apprehensively with him alongside for moral support. It must have been a shock for these men in their fifties and sixties to see the three of us walk up. All of us had shoulder-length hair and were wearing T-shirts, jeans, and sandals. They asked us what we wanted prayer for and Bob immediately said that we wanted to receive the baptism in the Holy Spirit. Actually, I just wanted to get it over with.

John went first because there was no way I was going

to. In what seemed to be an instant, John was speaking in strange syllables at the top of his lungs. I looked at Bob and he was grinning from ear to ear. So were the four men who were standing over him. (I could only imagine what that poor woman was thinking.) Then after a few moments of taking what happened all in, they looked at me. I gingerly approached the chair not knowing what in the world to expect. Again, in what seemed to be a few mere moments, I was praying in similar strange syllables with tears streaming down my face.

When it was all over I felt ecstatic. This changed everything. No longer was this some new teaching that I may or may not follow in the months to come. Following Jesus was real. At that moment, I couldn't explain what had happened to me, but I knew it was something real and amazing. It hit me that this was the first time I had cried since Dad's funeral when I was being restrained by my relatives. After we left, Bob, John, and I split up. I walked the two miles or so to my house knowing that it was time to tell Mom and Alice about Jesus. John and I were not the only ones with a story to tell however. Those four men and two ladies went home with a story to tell of their own.

Mom and Alice

It was sometime about midnight or so that I returned home. Mom, as usual, was waiting for me to get home. She asked me where I had been, fully expecting the same evasive or otherwise non-informative answer I had always given her. This time would prove to be different. Mom received the shock of her life. I simply asked her to sit down and I calmly began to tell her my story.

Since the house was small, it was not hard for Alice to hear what was going on. Somewhere in the middle of my story, I remember Alice coming in, sitting down, and taking it all in. I gave Mom an honest overview of my life leading up to the afternoon six days earlier when I had my life-changing encounter. I spared little detail when describing my drug use and overall risky lifestyle. Finally, I described my encounter with the gospel, my prayer receiving Jesus as my Lord and Savior six days before, and my experience that night.

Mom was more stunned than anything after hearing my story. It is important to understand that Mom's ties to the Jewish faith were more matters of history and tradition than anything else. It is also vital to understand how deep her fears were when it came to what others thought, most especially her mother, Grandma Salter. She immediately understood what the response of the family, our two Jewish neighbors the Behrigs, and the members of the Sons of Jacob would be.

I recall her saying a couple of things. She asked why I needed Jesus to change my life. After I repeated elements of my story to her and reminded her of where I was headed, Mom expressed her greatest concern. She pleaded with me to never tell anyone in the family, especially Grandma. It would kill her, she said in an impassioned and exaggerated tone.

I was not unsympathetic to Mom's concerns for a couple of reasons. First of all, I did not relish a confrontation with Grandma, the extended family, the neighbors, or anyone else. Secondly, I did not want to hurt my grandmother or affect her heath in any adverse way. Finally, my main priority at that moment was to allow my own life to stabilize. It had been less than a week since that afternoon in Bob's bedroom and I was still making sense of it myself.

At the end of the conversation, I made Mom a promise. I would not go out of my way to tell Grandma, but neither would I deny or lie. My response was not totally satisfactory to Mom or even myself for that matter. It was clear to me that silence would not be sustainable. It would however buy me time. I resolved to leave it in the hands of God. He would do what was best.

When I went to bed, I realized that so much had changed and yet so much was unresolved. Trust in God for whatever reason was not difficult however. I could only wonder what was in the mind of Mom and Alice. Mom, I suppose, was relieved in one sense that my life had moved from its destructive course, but in another sense, was fearful of a whole set of new possibilities. Alice was largely very quiet. As I would later learn, she was simply watching and listening intently.

A Fledgling Community

In the days that followed, my time was increasingly occupied with Bob, John, and Sue. Our time together was spent gathering to pray, learning from the Bible (Bob was a very capable teacher and disciple-maker), and singing songs about Jesus as Bob played guitar. We would also go to "The Wall" and talk to friends from time to time.

During this time, I found myself becoming closer to Bob, John, and Sue than I had with anyone I could remember. It was a wholly unique bond. Bob would use the terms "brother and sister in Christ" to describe our relationships with one another, and that is precisely how we felt. We cared for each other in ways none of us had ever previously experienced. Bob, John, Sue, and I were becoming a primitive faith community.

Our small, but soon to be growing, community was crucial to the development of our newly acquired faith. During this initial period of our spiritual journeys, we prayed for each other continuously, shared our struggles concerning our families, worshipped together, and held one another accountable. We also learned how to share our faith. All of these things became regular and vital parts of our daily living. God was using each of us to establish His incredible saving work in one another's lives.

Chapter 12
Confusion and Growth

"For this reason, since the day we heard about you, we have not stopped praying for you. We continually ask God to fill you with the knowledge of his will through all the wisdom and understanding that the Spirit gives, so that you may live a life worthy of the Lord and please him in every way: bearing fruit in every good work, growing in the knowledge of God."
—Colossians 1:9–10

"You, Lord, keep my lamp burning;
my God turns my darkness into light.
With your help I can advance against a troop;
with my God I can scale a wall."
—Psalm 18:29

"Therefore, my dear friends, as you have always obeyed—not only in my presence, but now much more in my absence—continue to work out your salvation with fear and trembling, for it is God who works in you to will and to act in order to fulfill his good purpose."
—Philippians 2:12–13

Things were changing so incredibly fast. Everything was radically new. There were no halfway measures, only radical choices to give Jesus everything. My initial instinct was to bargain with God, only to hear Bob's unrelenting challenge to give Jesus *everything*. Even when I considered the Ten Commandments, I recall offering to keep eight or nine out of ten, only to read Jesus' words, "Anyone who sets aside one of the least of these commands and teaches others accordingly will be called least of the kingdom of heaven" (Matthew 5:19). It seemed obvious to me that neither Bob nor the Lord would allow me any slack.

Spiritual growth is the work of the Holy Spirit and not that of any person. It is also true however that the person must cooperate with the Spirit in order for His work to come to fruition. Scripture makes clear that God is the initiator and the person is the responder. While there will undoubtedly be challenges along the way that will test and prove the individual, the Lord will be faithful to complete the work of the kingdom of God in the person's life.

Looking back, I can see over and again the hand of God from the earliest days of my new life. There were many bumps and bruises along the way, but the Lord was with me prompting, leading, and enabling at every point. The early months were especially confusing, but were also months of tremendous spiritual growth.

The Group Expands

For a couple of months our excursions to "The Wall" and other places where people our age hung out bore little fruit. Multiple times each week we would faithfully share the gospel with friends and acquaintances, only to find precious little response. People would for the most part tolerate our presence but that was just about it. On occasion, we would find some conversation and interest but few if any takers when it came to the good news we were offering.

All of that began to change in January 1971. A former classmate of mine, Steve Espamer, returned to Vineland after spending one semester at the University of Alaska in Fairbanks. I remember him riding in town on a motorcycle with a Captain America helmet and leather fringe jacket. He ran into Bob, John, and me almost immediately after his arrival. We shared the gospel with him and before long he committed his life to Jesus.

In addition to Steve, other friends and acquaintances began to respond. Our group started to grow little by little. We learned of others from nearby communities who came to faith in Christ through what would later be called the Jesus Movement and connected with them. Two young Jewish believers named Lynn and Lorie who lived in Philadelphia were introduced to Bob and from time to time visited our group. Others from Pennsville and Bridgeton, New Jersey, joined us more often. Bolstered by these visiting brothers and sisters, our group at times outgrew the houses in which we would meet.

One day our group experienced a completely unexpected addition. After coming home from one of our group gatherings, I was prompted to invite my sister Alice to one of our services. Oddly, it had not occurred to me that she might be interested enough in what had happened to me to seriously consider Jesus. It turned out that she was far more interested than I had realized. She had been watching quietly what had taken place in my life and had somehow become intrigued with what she had seen. Amazingly that day she received Christ as her Lord and Savior. God had made His first inroads into my family.

Bad Theology and Power Trips

As our group grew, some serious problems began to manifest. The most significant of these had to do with our leader,

Bob. It seemed that the more our numbers increased, the more Bob was determined to control what members of the group did. He began to teach us that the Holy Spirit gave witness to our own spirit concerning God's will relating to the specific decisions we needed to make. He taught us that although all of us were capable of receiving "the Spirit's witness," he as leader would receive this leading more often. His "witness of the Spirit" ultimately overrode our own senses of the Holy Spirit's leading. As the days and weeks went by, his control over the smallest of our decisions began to increase. Before long, it reached a level that became hard to take.

John, Steve Espamer, and I began to question this control. On one occasion, Steve and I decided to speak with Harry Snook, the pastor of Chestnut Assembly of God, to ask whether or not our understanding of how God worked was consistent with what the Bible taught. It was Pastor Snook who laid his hands on me when I received the baptism in the Holy Spirit. The two of us felt we could trust and confide in this man.

One afternoon we knocked on his door and his wife Ella answered. She invited us in and we spent more than an hour describing our Holy Spirit theology to Pastor Harry. We told him we believed we should not do anything until the Holy Spirit prompted us by giving a witness. He asked if that meant "anything," and we responded yes. He then asked us how we knew when we received these witnesses, and we told him we would usually receive a confirmation in the form of a shiver or other similar sensation. The more we described it, the more he laughed. He had truly never heard anything like it.

Steve and I mentioned to him that Bob received the strongest witnesses and we almost always submitted to his sense of what the Holy Spirit was saying. It didn't take long for Pastor Harry to recognize our predicament. He sensed that we were being dominated by Bob and were increasingly becoming victims of his desire to control our lives. Pastor Harry opened the Bible and began to teach us what it meant to be led by the Spirit. He explained that all of us could read the Bible for ourselves and be taught by God. He also helped us to see that it was important for us to learn how to perceive the voice of the Lord.

The two of us left Pastor Harry's living room feeling a new sense of freedom. We began reading the Bible more intently and understanding it in a greater dimension. It was not long before Steve, John, Sue, and I took significant responsibility for our own spiritual growth and relationship with the Lord.

New Spiritual Influences

The combination of Pastor Harry's liberating teaching and our own growing dissatisfaction with Bob's controlling style ultimately led us to seek more stable spiritual leadership. Virtually all of the members of our group eventually cut our ties to Bob and we began to attend Chestnut Assembly. In doing so, we exposed ourselves to the organized church for the first time. Like many, if not most people in the early days of the Jesus Movement, we harbored an instinctive distrust of organized Christianity in general and the institutional church in particular.

Fortunately for us however, Pastor Harry's unique personality and deep spiritual commitment made this transition easier for us than it would be for most. It also helped that he regularly gave us a tremendous amount of his personal time and energy. It seemed as though it didn't matter how many questions we had or how much time we required, Pastor Harry treated us as if we were his highest priorities. There was simply never a time that he was too busy to talk.

I recall the first Sunday we decided to come to the church to attend a service. We walked in amidst the stares of the members of the congregation and proceeded to walk down the church aisle to take our place in the first two rows of the auditorium. Everyone knows that the first two rows of a church auditorium are nearly always uninhabited. We could never figure out why no one wanted a front row seat to witness what God was doing. It would be easy to understand why everyone in the church stared. In that day people in their late teens with long hair, T-shirts, and jeans did not march into churches and sit in front pews. We were certainly quite the spectacle.

As it happened, the people of the congregation were not the only ones in for a surprise. The music, singing, and expressive joy of a Pentecostal church were nothing we had experienced before. In addition, we sensed the Spirit of God in that church sanctuary. Pastor Harry and a number of the people in the church welcomed us with affection. While there were many who were apprehensive at our presence, we didn't notice it at the time. We simply reveled in the presence of God and the unusual reality that people who were so unlike us would receive us so gladly.

Sunday after Sunday, we took our place on the front pews of the church sanctuary. After a short while, we took up three rows of pews instead of two and then four instead of three and before long we filled half of the church. The more often we came, the more it seemed that people were excited to see us. Again that was not true of everyone, but we were oblivious to any adverse reaction there was. God had given us a new home and we had received a very large adoptive family.

Overcoming through Determination

As far as my life was concerned, I was growing spiritually in many respects but struggling in others. I could not get enough of studying the Bible, my newfound relationships, and attending Chestnut Assembly. I could not wait for Sundays. Most of the time, I would not have to. Steve, John, and I would make up excuses to "bother" Pastor Harry. We would hang around the church hoping to run into him. On numerous occasions he would take us to a diner, and we would talk about what it meant to follow Jesus.

While my knowledge of the Bible and commitment to love and serve Jesus was growing, a great deal of my life was still in a state of shambles. I failed three of my college classes and received a fortunate D in a fourth during the fall of 1970. Attending college did not seem to fit in with my new life. I just did not get the significance of things that did not directly impact my spiritual walk. So in the spring of 1971, I decided to drop out of school and get a job. The only problem was jobs were not plentiful for anyone, let alone people like me with few life or job skills.

I did eventually find a job as an assistant washman in the laundry at Newcomb Hospital in Vineland. My job was to assist the person responsible for washing all the bloody and soiled sheets, dirty towels, and other linens of the hospital patients. I almost immediately realized how I got hired. This was not the kind of job people were standing in line for. The washman was an odd man with a volatile temper. He would yell and scream at me when things did not go well, only to apologize afterwards. He constantly complained of headaches and that made me think something was seriously wrong with him.

My suspicions were confirmed after about three weeks on the job. One day, I came to work only to find out that the washman had experienced a brain hemorrhage and had to have emergency surgery. Later, I learned that he survived the surgery but would be no longer able to work. The supervisor called me in and told me that his job was now mine, and they would try to find me an assistant to take my place. That person, for whatever reason, was never hired.

In the weeks that went by, I did my best to provide the clean laundry for the female workers whose job was to fold the sheets, pillowcases, towels, and other linens. I simply could not do it fast enough and the workers ended up standing around with little to do. I was warned that I needed to work harder and faster. I did my best, but the situation did not improve. Finally one day, the supervisor called me into his office and told me that I would be terminated. Someone from another department with experience would take my place.

I was devastated, not because I desired the job as hospital washman, but because I felt that it was a bad reflection on Jesus for me to fail in this way. When I sat in the supervisor's office and received the news, I did something startling. For the lack of a better way of saying it, I refused to be fired. You may ask, how does a person refuse to be fired? The answer is a person simply refuses to leave the office until the supervisor allows him to have a second chance (or in my case a third or fourth chance because I had been warned). I told him that I was a new Christian and I wanted to do a good job and would do anything I could to prove myself. He told me that he could not keep me because he had received so many complaints about not having the clean laundry necessary to keep the hospital functioning. He went on to say that he was sorry and acknowledged that it was not entirely my fault. I simply had proven myself unable to perform what the job required. I was unrelenting, however. I promised to prove him and the other workers wrong, and pleaded for one more chance. Having never encountered such resistance to firing someone, he ultimately relented and gave me three days to prove him wrong.

I prayed for the ability to bring God glory. I am convinced to this very day that He supernaturally gave me the power to work beyond my ability. I literally raced around like a mad man compensating for my lack of efficiency with extraordinary effort. Amazingly, the women who folded the laundry began to receive just enough to keep things going. Each day I got more efficient and each day the workers had more laundry to fold. I never heard another word from the supervisor. I kept that job for five more months until I decided that I did not want to be a hospital laundryman my entire life. When I gave my supervisor my two weeks' notice, he told me how sorry he was that I was leaving and how impressed he was with my determination. When it was all over, I had glorified God and learned the meaning of hard work.

Late during the summer of 1971, I decided that I would return to Cumberland County College and resume my education. I applied as I had before only to experience another surprise. I was not accepted. It seems that my terrible high school record combined with my 0.25 grade point average (three Fs and a D) during the previous fall semester had convinced the admissions office that I was incapable of doing college work, even at a community college.

My experience with the supervisor at Newcomb Hospital had taught me an invaluable lesson however. I could, as I did before, refuse to not be accepted for admission. I determined to march into the office of the person responsible for declining my admission and promise to prove him and the "powers that be" wrong, if they would only give me a second chance. I pleaded for one more semester to prove that I was capable of college work. I told him that my life had been changed because of Jesus, and He would give me the ability to succeed.

The admissions counselor tried to convey to me that my grades in high school and college had demonstrated an inability to do college work. My record of failure had convinced the Admissions Department that I would be unable to succeed. As he apologized and told me that his hands were tied, I just sat there. I reiterated that I would prove myself if I just had another chance. The more he tried to persuade me to seek other goals, the more determined I became. In the end, I outlasted him. I'm sure he realized that the only way to get me out of his office was to relent and give me one more opportunity.

Steve Espamer and I went to school together during the fall of 1971 and that was a good thing. He had a car and I did not. We competed with each other during that semester and that too was a good thing. When the semester was over we both made the President's List. To qualify for the President's List, you needed to have a 3.75 grade point average.

I never saw the admissions counselor again and I sometimes wonder if he checked to see how I did. I hope so. I was learning the value of a strong work ethic and the importance of giving God my best.

Chapter 13
Family Shock

"Blessed are you when people insult you, persecute you and falsely say all kinds of evil against you because of me. Rejoice and be glad, because great is your reward in heaven, for in the same way they persecuted the prophets who were before you."
—Matthew 5:11–12

"Whoever acknowledges me before others, I will also acknowledge before my Father in heaven. But whoever disowns me before others, I will disown before my Father I heaven. Do not suppose that I have come to bring peace to the earth. I did not come to bring peace, but a sword. For I have come to turn a man against his father, a daughter against her mother, a daughter-in-law against her mother-in-law—a man's enemies will be the members of his own household. Anyone who loves their father or mother more than me is not worthy of me; anyone who loves their son or daughter more than me is not worthy of me. Whoever does not take up their cross and follow me is not worthy of me. Whoever finds their life will lose it, and whoever loses their life for my sake will find it."
—Matthew 10:32–39

Sooner or later they will have to find out." I told myself over and over that it was in God's hands. My heart was torn between my Grandmother's need to hear the gospel and the anticipated turmoil the news of my faith in Jesus would bring. I possessed no desire for the rejection, hostility, and the certain unrelenting pain in the lives of others that would accompany this new spiritual reality in my life.

Jesus said there would be times when our loyalty to Him would cost us. Often the place where this happens is our families. Commitment to Jesus Christ on occasion will bring discord to our relationships with those whom we love the most. The pain of family division can be among the most significant we experience.

Our Lord knew both the likelihood of family persecution and depth of the potential hurt. In fact, He predicted that it would occur. He was aware of the cost many who loved Him would have to bear, and promised that it would not go unrewarded. It is often the believer's greatest test.

The First Phase of Family Shock

The potential separation from members of my family because of my faith was something I knew that I would have to face. I was aware of it from the beginning. How my grandmother and extended family members would react to my faith in Christ was pretty much a foregone conclusion. Mom's concerns as I noted previously were mostly about this potential response. She didn't want her mother hurt or the contention that would be inevitable. She simply hoped vainly that I would keep it quiet.

For my part, I was biding my time and delaying the inevitable. Deep within me there was a sense that the news would get out and more likely sooner than later. I just didn't know the circumstances through which it would take place. In my grandmother's presence I would never have to bring the subject up, so I simply avoided it. All the while I was praying that God would bring about the time and circumstances.

The time and circumstances came soon enough. In the year

that followed my spiritual transformation, the Lord had begun doing incredible things in Vineland. Those of us who came to faith were sharing Jesus with people we knew on a daily basis. Teenagers our age were coming to the Lord in ever-increasing numbers. That first year the number exceeded a hundred, and news was gradually spreading in the community as a result of testimony after testimony of young people being delivered from drugs.

The local paper, the *Vineland Times Journal* as it was called then, heard of what was happening and called Pastor Harry, asking to interview him along with a representative number of transformed teenagers. Pastor Harry arranged the event and, you guessed it, I was among those selected to be interviewed. One reporter showed up that afternoon along with a photographer. After it was over, I simply sighed and prayed to myself, "Thy will be done." I knew it was in the hands of God.

The next day, I arose early and looked for the article. It was not there. Maybe, I thought, the paper would not view the life transformations of teenagers as worthy of one of its feature stories. But when the paper arrived the day after, there it was for all to see. It was a front-page story that was continued on two of the inside pages. The actual names of those interviewed were exchanged for fictitious ones, but my description was unmistakable. In the article I was called "Joe" and described as "prematurely gray at the age of 19." There was also an accompanying picture, a side view, but clear enough. To make matters worse (or better, depending on your perspective), the accompanying picture appeared on the paper's front page just below the fold. I braced myself and just waited.

I didn't have to wait long. I hadn't told Mom of the interview but she found out when the phone rang late that afternoon. It was Grandma Salter and she was screaming. I could hear her across the living room. She did not see the paper herself at first, but one of the ladies from the Sons of Jacob Sisterhood recognized me from the picture and the accompanying description.

A Jewish boy becoming a follower of Jesus was a shock and a tragedy in a Jewish community. I did not want to, but I had brought significant shame to my grandmother. She cried and pleaded with me. I told her that I did not want to hurt her and attempted to explain that Jesus had saved my life. Grandma wouldn't listen to anything I said, but only repeated again and again how ashamed she and everyone in the synagogue were of me. At least, I thought, I did not have to worry anymore about the time and circumstances.

A Kindly Encounter with a Rabbi

Any thought of this being over was soon dispelled. One day Mom received a call from my Orthodox Jewish neighbor Al Behrig. As I noted previously, Al Behrig lived next door to us while his brother Herb lived across the street. The Behrigs were kind to me after my father and grandfather died, and along with others, taught me the precepts of Orthodox Judaism. I was not home when he called, but Mom told me that a rabbi friend of theirs was interested in talking to me. As I recall, it was not the rabbi of the Sons of Jacob congregation but some other one.

A day or two later ,the rabbi called and I spoke with him. He was polite and asked if I would be willing to meet with him and I agreed. The meeting took place in Al Behrig's living room. It was a cordial meeting between the three of us, the rabbi, Al Behrig and me. Prior to the meeting, I did my best to ensure that I was prepared. I was already aware of the numerous Old Testament prophecies that spoke of the identity and circumstances of the coming Messiah's lineage, birth, ministry, suffering, atoning death, and resurrection. Additionally, in the approximate year since I had given my life to Jesus, I had become a diligent student of Scripture. I was as ready for the challenge as I could have possibly been.

I could only imagine the disappointment my grandmother, the Behrigs, and other members of the synagogue had felt. Only a few years prior, I had been a model, observant young Jewish boy. Now I had done the unthinkable. I had "converted to Christianity." For many Jews there is no greater betrayal than to abandon the faith of your heritage. Jews had endured persecution for centuries and that was an astonishing miracle in itself. Leaving your faith for another is to betray an incredibly meaningful and tremendous history.

Despite these deep emotions, the rabbi and Al Behrig were respectful and thoughtful. Only once that I can remember did the conversation border on accusation. I brought up two points in defense of my belief that Jesus was the long awaited Messiah of the Jewish people. First, I summed up the history of Israel in the Old Testament as primarily one of idolatry and spiritual failure rather than one of victory and faithfulness as I was taught as a child. I did so to establish that the Jewish people both then and now have had a deep spiritual need before God. Secondly, I focused on the many Old Testament prophecies, particularly those of the suffering Messiah for the nation's sins found in Isaiah chapters 52 and 53.

It was at these two points that the conversation got somewhat tense. The rabbi challenged both of these assertions stating unequivocally that I had become victimized by propaganda, which was typical of Christians who preyed upon uneducated Jewish people. Israel's Old Testament history was not characterized by idolatry, he maintained. He admitted that it was true they had some lapses but not to the degree I had been led to believe. When I challenged his assertion by stating that Israel had murdered a significant number of their own prophets in order to perpetuate their disobedience and rejection of God, he again vehemently denied that it was so.

In so far as my interpretation of the Isaiah passage was concerned, he challenged that as well. He stated the subject of the passage in question outlining suffering was not the Messiah but rather Israel. The correct interpretation, he maintained, was that it was referring to Israel's suffering for the world's sins and not the Messiah for Israel's.

I was startled by the rabbi's response to both of my main points of defense, and debated both his summary of Israel's ancient history and his interpretation of Isaiah. In the end we were both locked into our positions on the matters. When the evening ended, we were both respectful and cordial. He asked if I would be willing to meet again, and I agreed to do so. As I left, I was significantly aware of God's help and anointing. He had given me both the words to say and a respectful attitude. I felt as though I had represented Christ as well as a nineteen-year-old could be expected to.

It turned out that there would be no second meeting. I did receive a call from the rabbi attempting to schedule it, but for whatever reason the follow-up meeting didn't take place. I do remember the rabbi apologizing for an erroneous statement he had made. After researching the matter, he admitted that Israel had rejected and even killed a number of its prophets. As I recall, he didn't say more. For me the implication was obvious. Old Testament Israel had a deep spiritual need, one that the rabbi, if he was honest, had to acknowledge. I took it as a vindication of my faith.

When the affair was over, my confidence increased at two levels. I had experienced divine help when I had been challenged to defend my faith in Jesus. These experiences should be treasured because they are markers that can be built upon.

We should treat them as "stones of remembrance" in the same way they were treated by people of old (Joshua 4:4–9).

My confidence had been enhanced in another way as well. It was becoming clear to me that I was growing strong in my faith at a number of levels. I was beginning to feel that I could hold my own against even learned, educated individuals. Self-confidence is not a bad thing within limits. I was learning that there was a difference between self-confidence and self-sufficiency. This was important because at this early stage of my Christian faith, I still possessed deep wounds that left me needing substantial emotional and psychological healing.

Family Shock: Part Two

It is fair to say that Grandma Salter's response to my faith in Jesus evolved over time. It became a work in progress. My grandmother loved me deeply and although she was devastated and shamed over the transition that was taking place in my life, she could not bring herself to disown either Alice or me. Grandma was left to damage control. Locals knowing what had happened to us was one thing, the rest of the family finding out was another. Just as Mom begged me not to tell Grandma Salter, she begged me to keep it from the rest of the family. Since all her close relatives lived in Philadelphia approximately an hour from Vineland, and since the family did not get together as often as it once did, this didn't seem to be too difficult a prospect.

When I was younger I seem to remember family gatherings on a near annual basis. Our family's tragedies changed all that. As the family got older and experienced transitions, these times were much less frequent. I can only remember one large family get together during my teen years.

One day Grandma Salter told us that a family gathering was going to take place at the home of my Aunt Esther and Uncle Harry Berkowitz in north Philly. Aunt Esther was my grandmother's niece and her husband Harry was by far the most devoutly Orthodox of anyone in the family. My grandmother implored me to not say anything about my commitment to Jesus. Reluctantly, I promised.

Since my sister and I were the only ones in the family who had a driver's license, one of us had to drive. Alice had a lime green Ford Pinto that she had purchased just a few months prior. The plan was for us to drive to Aunt Esther and Uncle Harry's home where we would meet members of the family we had not seen in some time. Along with my immediate family, Aunt Esther and Uncle Harry, my Uncle Leo (Mom's twin brother) and his wife Rae, my Aunt Pauline and Uncle Harry Follack, my Aunt Mary and Uncle Harry Moss (we had a lot of Uncle Harrys in the family) were present. There were also others present as well, but who they were I don't recall.

The night before we were to leave for the family reunion, I remembered a chilling detail I had forgotten. After purchasing the lime green Pinto, Alice and I had placed a matching lime green sticker on the rear bumper. It read "Jesus Loves You." I immediately realized that Alice and I were in the midst of a real dilemma. What do we do? Removing the bumper sticker represented denying my faith. I just couldn't do that for any reason. Alice and I decided to leave it on, not tell my grandmother and mother, and hope that no one saw it. I just put in the hands of God and left the whole matter to Him.

When we arrived at the north Philadelphia Jewish neighborhood, most, if not all of the family had already gotten there. Honestly, my immediate thought was that was a good thing because no one would have to go behind Alice's car and see the bumper sticker. I didn't want a confrontation or to shame my grandmother before the family. I wanted to be the first to leave and the revelation of my faith to be for another time and place. It seemed as though my desires would be honored. The afternoon went by quickly and uneventfully. We finished our dinner and I recommended to Mom and Grandma that we leave before too long since we had a relatively long trip ahead of us. It was not really long, perhaps about an hour and a half from the part of north Philly we were in but certainly a reasonable request. It looked as if Alice and I would make it out unscathed.

That was until my Uncle Harry Berkowitz decided to take out the trash. Trash pickup, it turned out, was the next day. I had no idea he was doing so (if I did, I probably would have offered to do it). The next thing I knew Uncle Harry was yelling loud enough for everyone to hear. He came out of the garage with an axe and threated to hack the car into pieces. My Aunt Esther was holding him back.

When the dust had settled, everyone found out the reason for Uncle Harry's agitated state. He had seen the bumper sticker and knew it belonged to Alice and me. In a few minutes Uncle Harry was threatening me, Grandma was crying, Mom was yelling, "How could you?" and everyone was looking at me for an explanation. This must have been how Peter and John felt when they were before the Sanhedrin, I thought.

At that moment, I remember feeling a supernatural calm as I began to share my story of the years that followed the deaths of Dad and Grand Pop Salter. They sat quietly as I told of my years at the Sons of Jacob Synagogue and subsequent years of searching and drug use. When I was done it seemed as though everyone left the room. No one wanted to be around Alice or me. As far as nearly everyone was concerned, we had betrayed anything and everything they held dear. I remember only one of my relatives talking to me the rest of the time we were there. My Aunt Pauline Follack sat down with me and asked me questions. To my memory, she was always kind to Alice and me. Even though she was calm and kind, it was clear that she didn't approve. The only other person who didn't reject us on that day was my Uncle Leo, Mom's brother. That would have been totally out of character for him.

We left perhaps an hour or so after the blowup. We were in the back of the driveway blocking everyone else, so that turned out to be a good excuse to leave when we did. As far as everyone else was concerned, especially Uncle Harry Berkowitz, our leaving was undoubtedly a relief. Alice and I would not see most of these relatives ever again. A few showed up at Grandma Salter's funeral (more about this later). Much later I would be able to establish a somewhat meaningful relationship with my Uncle Leo and Aunt Rae, but otherwise no one in the extended family would ever contact Alice and me again.

The trip home was the quietest hour and a half I can ever remember spending. Very early during the trip, I remember Grandma crying and promising to never forgive me. That thankfully was a promise she would not nor could not keep. Grandma Salter loved Alice and me too much to never forgive us. I thank God there is more of Grandma Salter's story to tell. For my part, the lack of conversation in the car provided me with an opportunity to think—and praise God. On the one hand, I felt very sad for my grandmother. The last thing I wanted to do was hurt her. My grandmother was truly a very special person. On the other hand however, I found myself rejoicing deep down. I had been faithful to God. True, there was some reluctance on my part to expose myself to the family strife that resulted. I realized even then however, that

God does not measure our reluctance. He measures what we do and our motives behind what we do.

As the four of us drove home in that very quiet lime green Ford Pinto, I had an untouchable joy, one that proved true the last of the Beatitudes found in Matthew's account of the Sermon on the Mount: "Blessed are those who are persecuted because of righteousness, for theirs is the kingdom of heaven" (5:10). I vaguely remembered that there was another promise for those who chose to love Jesus more than anyone else: "Truly I tell you . . . . no one who has left home or brothers or sisters or mother or father or children or fields for me and the gospel will fail to receive a hundred times as much in this present age: homes, brothers, sisters, mothers, children and fields—along with persecutions—and in the age to come eternal life" (Mark 10:29–30).

Chapter 14
A Special Place

"They devoted themselves to the apostles' teaching and to fellowship, to the breaking of bread and to prayer. Everyone was filled with awe at the many wonders and signs performed by the apostles. All the believers were together and had everything in common. They sold property and possessions to give to anyone who had need. Every day they continued to meet together in the temple courts. They broke bread in their homes and ate together with glad and sincere hearts, praising God and enjoying the favor of all the people. And the Lord added to their number daily those who were being saved."

—Acts 2:42–47

"Let the peace of Christ rule in your hearts, since as members of one body you were called to peace. And be thankful. Let the message of Christ dwell among you richly as you teach and admonish one another with all wisdom through psalms, hymns, songs from the Spirit, singing to God with gratitude in your hearts."

—Colossians 3:15–16

The early days of the Christian Church were marked by a fervor that has stood out as unique throughout church history. The first Christians recognized the critical importance of the apostles' teaching, a vibrant, believing community, worship, prayer, and reaching their fellow Jews with the gospel. Their daily way of life was characterized by a deep love for one another and a purity of heart that has not since been replicated. As a result, God moved mightily in their midst and the Church multiplied daily. Thousands were added to their ranks in a very short period of time.

I do not claim that my early Christian experience was in any way the same as the experience of Christ's initial followers. My experience and that of my newly found brothers and sisters did not consist of the lame walking or the blind receiving their sight. Nor did it involve the selling of our possessions and the communal holding of all our material belongings. Our first few years did not include multiplied thousands coming to the faith. It did however include a number of similarities to what was experienced in the early chapters of the Book of Acts.

What took place in my life from late 1970 to the fall of 1973 was incredibly formational. Unquestionably, it was the closest thing I have ever experienced to the Early Church model and remarkable in so many different dimensions. During the first three years of my Christian experience, I participated in a move of God that forever shaped the man I would become. I look back on those days longingly because they were so precious in that I was experiencing God's transforming power in an accelerated fashion.

A Place of Instruction

During the early years of my spiritual development, I was a sponge when it came to the Word of God. There was no such thing as church once, twice, or even three times a week. Every day we were either at Chestnut Assembly of God or in one another's homes with the Bible open and our hearts pliable to what we would read. As far as my friends and I were concerned, the Bible had complete authority over our lives.

We were much more likely to go overboard than entertain the slightest compromise. We were all in.

As explained earlier, after the first few months John Wilhelm, Sue Griffith, Steve Espamer, and the others that joined us gradually and increasingly gravitated from the mentoring of our former leader to that of Pastor Harry and the people of Chestnut Assembly of God. In the months that followed, the church began to grow rapidly. What was a congregation of just over a hundred or so when we arrived doubled in a short time, and grew more than fivefold in the three years that followed.

The church's numerical growth eventually led Pastor Harry to bring on additional staff, largely to aid in the discipleship of those from the sixties' drug culture who were occupying more and more pews from the front to the middle of the church sanctuary. While we were incredibly zealous, we were altogether untaught. That made us extremely vulnerable.

The staff reinforcements came in the form of Dwight and Nancy Colbaugh (Nancy was the daughter of Pastor Harry) and Roz and Sandy Flower. The Colbaughs and the Flowers were just a little older than most of us, and perfect fits for the job of making disciples of the growing band of hippie types who had changed the face of Chestnut Assembly almost overnight. But in many ways they too were stretched to their limit. We were spiritually hungry and required seemingly endless amounts of time and energy. Suffice it to say, my friends and I along with the many others who had come were in no way low maintenance.

Looking back, Harry and his wife Ella, the Colbaughs, and the Flowers had precious little time at their disposal that was not taken up with our endless needs. I don't know how they pulled it off. There was hardly a day when we were not occupying their time. We had questions—Bible questions, life questions, all kinds of questions. We had emotional issues, confidence issues, and, for some, even mental issues. Life had to be especially hard for these precious servants of God, and make no mistake, to us they were so very precious. We owe them a tremendous amount.

The Snooks, Colbaughs, and Flowers were bolstered by a not insignificant number of men and women from the Chestnut Assembly congregation. For my part, a large number of names and faces fill my memory. These include Don Breeden, Don Moe, Wayne Safford, Arthur Sutton, the Tates, the Powells, Marian Howell, and countless others. All these individuals hold special places in my heart. It seems the more I list the more I remember. I could fill paragraph after paragraph with more names.

When it came to teaching us the Bible, the venues were extremely varied. Every day it seemed, we would be learning somewhere and being taught by someone. Sunday mornings and Sunday evenings we would find ourselves listening to one of Pastor Harry's excellent sermons. Pastor Harry was what might be termed a "long-winded" preacher. A short sermon for Pastor Harry would be a little over an hour. His longer versions could go for an hour and a half or even longer. But we seldom if ever minded. Invariably, we would leave the sanctuary saying, "Wasn't it great?" His wife Ella would often caution him about the length of his sermons, but to no avail.

If we were not listening to Pastor Harry's sermons, we would be having Bible studies. Sometimes they were at the Snooks, Colbaughs or Flowers homes, or sometimes we had them on our own. Other venues for our discipleship included rap sessions on Friday evenings (more about these events later), conversations with our mentors, or dessert gatherings at the Presidential Diner located on the circle connecting Landis Avenue and Delsea Drive. Whenever or wherever they took place, none of us could get enough of God's Word. It was life to us.

A Place of Community

Perhaps the most life-giving element of my early years at Chestnut Assembly was the profound sense of community I experienced. When compared to my life prior to knowing Jesus as Lord and Savior that was characterized by intense loneliness, it was like the difference between night and day. On the family level, I had been deprived of a relationship with a father and a healthy one with a mother. As far as friends were concerned, relationships had been predicated on being considered cool even by those I considered closest. I was either alone by myself or alone in a crowd. Either way I always felt as if I were alone.

That all changed completely, when I came to faith in Jesus. Instead of few if any unconditional relationships, my life became full of countless ones. This was true of those who were my age and those who were much older. I often laughed at the fact I was close to so many I once would have considered "uncool" or "establishment." I was learning to be comfortable around people of all types. It was truly amazing.

It seemed as though every day was an opportunity to get together with someone, a few people, or a large group. It is easy to take for granted the numerous real and potential blessings related to being a part of such a believing community. It is equally easy to forget that most people have little or no such experience. People apart from Christ are often alone and isolated just as I once was. At the time, I had no such problem forgetting the way it used to be. It was obvious.

During the first three years of my Christian life, my closest friends were Steve Espamer and John Wilhelm. I spent long hours at their houses and came to know their parents, especially Steve's. The three of us were considered leaders among the ever-growing numbers of believers, partly because we were among the first and partly because of our perceived leadership qualities.

Steve and I were very competitive with each other on occasions. Both of us were insecure and in some sense found ourselves becoming rivals. It had to be comical to those observing us. Even though we were highly regarded by nearly everybody in the believing community, we both tried to be the highest regarded. Our spiritual growth and our spiritual immaturity seemed to take place simultaneously. We compared our prayer lives, our evangelistic efforts, and even competed to be the closest to Pastors Harry, Dwight, and Roz.

Despite it all however, we loved each other as brothers. Steve, John, and I realized we were part of something special. None of us ever imagined that we could be loved by so many people. Community for us was an everyday occurrence and a constant joy and resource to our lives.

A Place of Awe

The time between late 1970 and the fall of 1973 were also filled with events that left us awestruck. There is something about seeing God at work in the lives of large numbers of people that produces deep confidence for those who witness it. These times were full of dramatic testimonies, life transformations, and amazing occurrences. Wherever we went, we came to expect that God would do wonderful things.

During these years, church services were anything but routine. It was a very rare occurrence when at least someone did not make a new profession of faith following the sermon. In fact, there were times when individuals would not wait for the invitation to receive Christ at the conclusion of the service. I remember occasions when people would come forward to give their lives to Jesus during congregational singing or during the middle of the sermon. Nothing surprised us.

Needless to say, these occurrences were not limited to church services. Friday night rap sessions were also extraordinary events more times than not. Each Friday evening, teenagers and young adults would meet together in a building at the rear of the church property to discuss God and the Bible. The format was typically question and answer, but would nearly always deviate into something unplanned but ultimately fruitful. Early on, the gatherings would include a hundred or so young people. After time however, the sessions outgrew the hall and had to be moved to a different location. Eventually, we settled on Landis Park where there was a bandstand, which was ideal. Our relatively large crowd would ultimately draw a larger one because people would pass by and wonder what was going on. At its peak, the crowds would grow to two hundred or more.

In addition to witnessing God work through the numerous meetings that regularly took place, we watched Him work in our day-to-day lives. These years were characterized by a continual sense of the reality of God. Our faith was strong and faith brought expectation and expectation very often preceded some demonstration of God's presence.

I cannot explain why the Lord works powerfully in unique circumstances. That remains a mystery to me. I only know that these few short years still serve as reminders of what a move of the Spirit can look like. Nothing is more awesome than to witness prolonged periods of God at work.

A Place of Evangelism

For my friends and me, evangelism was a nearly everyday occurrence. We were ready "in season and out" (2 Timothy 4:2) to bring the good news of the life-changing power of God through Jesus. By that I mean we were ready when we participated in planned evangelistic outreaches (which were many and varied), and we were ready for impromptu opportunities. Two examples come to mind that illustrate these impromptu occasions.

Since I found myself walking to most places (Alice had the only car in the family at this time), I often interacted with people along my walking routes. On the way, it was common for me to stop and pick up snacks or something to tide me over in case I got hungry. I frequented two mom-and-pop establishments on a regular basis. One was called Esther & Pics and the other Casey's Market.

Esther & Pics was a typical, small family place where you could pick up milk, bread, eggs, and other items. The owners lived upstairs and the store occupied the first floor. In other circumstances, it would have been an inner-city, small, two-story home. Esther always sat by the cash register and was the only person I ever saw working in the establishment. She was a kindly Catholic woman who, for some reason, was interested in my well-being. Esther had witnessed me walking the streets over the years and genuinely cared about young people who struggled in life.

I remember one conversation with her at the checkout register, telling her about my recent commitment to Jesus. Her concerned expression turned into a smile as she stated that often she would worry about me when she saw me walking by the store. Instinctively, she knew that I was a troubled young person and in great need. I told her that although once I was deeply troubled and needy, I had experienced a radical life transformation. Esther would regularly ask me questions that provided me with a continual opportunity to share my faith. At times, others would be present as I shared my story and would listen intently to my description of the gospel and its power to change a person's life.

The same thing would take place at Casey's Market which was located on a different route. Casey was also a Catholic and was extremely interested and impressed with what was happening at Chestnut Assembly. Casey stated that he first learned of how God was changing the lives of hippies through the article that appeared in the *Vineland Times Journal* (the article that led to Grandma Salter and others discovering my new faith) and from time to time wondered if it was continuing. It seemed to me that whenever I entered the store, he made some attempt to talk with me and obtain the latest news about what was happening in the lives of these formerly needy teenagers. Doors continually opened for me to tell this religious Catholic man and others about how one could know God personally.

While there were many other encounters that were unplanned, others were more regular events that typically turned into unexpected evangelistic opportunities. Again, I will only describe a few of these in order to paint a picture of the significant evangelistic impact of these years. The first consistently took place after the rap sessions when they were moved to Landis Park. When the meetings concluded somewhat after ten p.m. on Friday evenings, many of us would hit Landis Avenue and begin talking with people about Jesus. Our approach was a simple one. We each would stop people, more often than not strangers, and ask a question like, "Do you have a couple of minutes to listen to something wonderful that has happened in my life?" At times, people would remark that by the time they got to us, they had already been stopped by two or three others. We would simply apologize and move on.

Once about eleven p.m. or so, four of us decided to get a

cup of coffee after we finished talking to people. Pastor Harry was driving and Steve, John, and I were in the car. As we approached the Presidential Diner, our favorite late-night hangout, the four of us noticed a hitchhiker and out of the blue decided to delay our coffee and pie in order to experience one more witnessing opportunity. We picked him up and asked him where he was going. He responded, "Anywhere. Just get me away from those Jesus freaks. They won't leave me alone." Once he got in the car, Pastor Harry just sped up and we told him that he was with four more. He was our captive for the more than twenty-minute trip to "anywhere."

A second regular weekly evangelistic event took place at Atlantic City, New Jersey. A local pastor secured a modestly sized outdoor pier on the famous Atlantic City Boardwalk. Being on the Boardwalk by the ocean would enable us to share with the literally hundreds of passersby. Microphones were set up, and our musicians would play and sing. My friends and I would share our testimonies. Most people would ignore us, but some would stop for a while and listen. As the ministry was taking place, some of our group would pass out gospel tracks with our church's address and phone number on the back. Certain people would take the time to listen to those of us who were "planted" in the audience.

People regularly prayed prayers of commitment. On occasion, we heard from others who contacted us later. Some of the stories were incredible. I remember one man who was literally running from the police for a previous offense. He wrote that he was convicted of his sin and gave his life to Christ. Afterward, the man decided to turn himself in to authorities and thanked us for sharing our message. We were able to contact the Atlantic City pastor who then ministered to the man in jail. We learned from the pastor that he was later granted probation and continued to serve the Lord along with his family.

Another situation involved a married couple who wrote and said they had received Jesus during our invitation after the boardwalk service. They stated that just before walking past the pier where our singing and testimonies were taking place, they had agreed to divorce. When they heard us sharing our stories of how Jesus had transformed our lives, they stopped to listen. After receiving Christ into their lives, they determined to give their marriage another chance. A month later they found the tract in a pocket and decided to thank us for making a difference in their lives.

Stories like this were not uncommon in those years. They were times of incredible expectancy. We witnessed the reality of God in and through our lives on an almost-daily basis. As I stated earlier, great things happen during times like this because they produce an expectation of God working which then produces an even-greater reality.

A Place of Healing

When it comes to the first three years or so of my new life, there is one more thing that must be said, especially as it relates to the impact the people of Chestnut Assembly had on my life personally. These people played a role in my emotional, psychological, and spiritual healing that they will never fully know. Even now as I write my story, I am filled with gratitude toward these men and women. It is a debt that I can never repay.

It would in some ways be wonderful if when we came to Christ the deepest wounds resulting from our participation in a world of sin and pain would immediately be healed. Unfortunately, of course, there is no delete button that can be hit to remove the consequences of our past. Healing must take place gradually as the Holy Spirit applies the necessary balm to our hurts. True, some wounds heal more quickly than others. For the most part however, these things take time as God's grace brings increasing wholeness.

My journey toward wholeness was greatly accelerated as a result of my involvement with so many loving, compassionate, and deeply caring individuals, the people of this wonderful congregation. Their love restored me in multiple ways. These people gave me a confidence in myself that, in itself, was a miracle. The day I came in contact with that congregation, I came as a person who not only lacked life skills, but also as one who saw himself as having little ability to become anything useful in life. They poured into me a sense of value. Only a small part of it was what they said to me. Far more important was the look in their eyes when I walked into their presence. This instilled in my life the first notion that I might be someone God could use.

Confidence when rightly placed is indispensable in life. Without it, we can do very little. In this world, people will either suck it from us or build it into the fiber of our beings. The people of this wonderful community of faith made it their determination to pour a sense of confidence, usefulness, and strength into the lives of a group of wayward young men and women who lacked it. I am sure that they never fully realized the value of what they were doing.

The people of Chestnut Assembly of God were not by and large educated, wealthy, or successful by the world's standards. They were the kind of people the apostle Paul was likely referring to when he wrote to the Corinthians, "Brothers and sisters, think of what you were when you were called. Not many of you were wise by human standards; not many were influential; not many were of noble birth" (1 Corinthians 1:26). But to me and many of my friends, they were the wisest, most influential, and most noble of people. They committed themselves to our well-being and I, for one, will never forget their faces. For whatever God has accomplished in my life in the years that followed, I owe much to these seemingly ordinary but utterly wonderful people. They were God's gifts to me in a time when they were so desperately needed.

Chapter 15
Christ Formed in Me

"His divine power has given us everything we need for a godly life through our knowledge of him who called us by his own glory and goodness. Through these he has given us his very great and precious promises, so that through them you may participate in the divine nature, having escaped the corruption in the world caused by evil desires.

"For this very reason, make every effort to add to your faith goodness; and to goodness, knowledge; and to knowledge, self-control; and to self-control, perseverance; and to perseverance, godliness; and to godliness, mutual affection; and to mutual affection, love. For if you possess these qualities in increasing measure, they will keep you from being ineffective and unproductive in your knowledge of our Lord Jesus Christ. But whoever does not have them is nearsighted and blind, forgetting that they have been cleansed from their past sins.

"Therefore, my brothers and sisters, make every effort to confirm your calling and election. For if you do these things, you will never stumble, and you will receive a rich welcome into the eternal kingdom of our Lord and Savior Jesus Christ."

—2 Peter 1:3–11

The extraordinary first couple of years at Chestnut Assembly also provided me stark lessons about how God works in the lives of people. I witnessed so many people come to faith in Christ and watched some experience dramatic conversions. Many of these individuals continued in the faith and grew rapidly. Others however seemed to flounder and struggle, leaving their first love only to return to their previous lives of drug use or worse. There were times when it was unclear which was larger, the front door where people came to new life or the back door where people returned to their old ways.

Don't get me wrong. Watching God work in these exciting years was absolutely unforgettable. The authenticity of peoples' life commitments left me with an incredible appreciation of divine power. But at times it also left me with feelings of disappointment. It was sad to see people begin with passionate faith only to give it all back for some inexplicable reason. It wasn't easy to grasp all that was going on. As time passed, I began to have reoccurring concerns about the future of my own spiritual journey. Would I continue to grow or would I become shipwrecked like some others I knew?

Perspectives on Spiritual Growth

Before continuing with my story, I feel the need to offer some crucial perspectives on how believers grow spiritually. I have always been incredibly blessed by the many varied individuals divinely placed in my path who helped disciple me. These individuals spoke into my life critical spiritual principles that enabled me to grow.

I would like to begin by emphasizing spiritual growth is not an option for those who consider themselves to be followers of Jesus Christ. True faith in Christ requires a serious and determined attitude. Believers who lack this attitude are certain to encounter increasing difficulties in their walk with Christ. When they fail to go forward, they will certainly find themselves falling backward.

It is also essential to realize that Christian maturity cannot be achieved by mere human effort and striving. It is a partnership between a faithful and determined heart and the resources provided by God himself. Neither can take effect without the other. It is critical therefore that we recognize the potential consequences of failing to embrace the biblical imperative for our spiritual growth.

Our responsibility is to personally embrace this imperative. Our free will continues to exist after our initial profession of faith. We remain free to pursue the Lord and to determine the extent of that pursuit.

We must recognize that our spiritual maturity will not occur by accident. We have a determined spiritual foe who day and night strategizes to hinder us in every possible way (2 Corinthians 2:11; 1 Peter 5:8). In addition to the schemes of Satan, as followers of Christ we must wrestle against our own fallen nature that is vulnerable to sin and its allures. Temptation is something believers will always need to resist while on this earth. Overconfidence must be resisted and replaced by dependence upon the Spirit of God.

Lordship demands an unequivocal loyalty to Jesus Christ. Our faithfulness will provide the ultimate evidence of our faith. That does not mean that we will never fall short from time to time. It does however mean that we will resolve to grow into the likeness and character of Christ and allow nothing to keep us from this end. Spiritual growth is not a mere option for us.

The apostle Peter summarizes the imperative of spiritual growth in 2 Peter 1:3–11. In this passage he emphasizes God's provision and the requirement of the disciple's cooperation. Both are required in order for genuine discipleship to take place.

It is God who has given us everything we need to grow into the fullness of Christian maturity. The Holy Spirit lives within us for the purpose of developing the divine nature. This is accomplished by an ever-increasing knowledge of Christ. The more we participate in the divine nature the more we find ourselves able to escape the corruption that is in the world (vs. 3–4). It is God who supplies the strength and ability to make His ultimate will for our lives a reality.

Peter, however, calls believers to "make every effort" to cooperate with the divine power that enables them. God supplies the power, but we must supply the effort and determination. Peter lists crucial virtues necessary to growing in the character of Jesus Christ our Lord. These virtues have a necessary and important order to them. We must make every effort to add goodness to our faith, then knowledge, self-control, perseverance, godliness, mutual affection, and love.

Peter concludes this passage with a promise to those who cooperate with God's power at work in their lives. The pursuit of the character of Christ will bring great reward. Obedient disciples will be effective and productive as they seek to bring increase to the kingdom of God.

It is important to give attention to the conditional nature of the promise. The qualities that depict kingdom character must exist in the lives of Christ's disciples and exist in increasing measure. The qualities themselves act as a guarantee against spiritual failure. Progressive spiritual growth is the best protection against spiritual decline. Believers must keep on moving forward in their walk with God.

Peter's promise of blessing is followed by a warning in verse 9. He admonishes that all who lack the aforementioned qualities are nearsighted and blind. Those who are nearsighted cannot see things far away. They lack the ability to see past the immediate. Nearsighted people are unable to foresee the long-term consequences of their behavior and are doomed to reap the temporal and eternal ramifications of their foolish living.

In short, people who claim to be followers of Jesus and lack the progressive character qualities that reflect the One they claim to follow lack wisdom. Wisdom can be defined as the ability to see the end at the beginning. Examples of this abound in life. Those who are addicted to sinful behaviors never thought they would become addicted when they began engaging in sin. Alcoholics never foresaw their condition when they took their first drink. Drug addicts likewise, did not perceive their enslavement to drugs when they first partook. Similarly, professing believers who deceive themselves into believing they can partake in sin and not be ultimately affected lack wisdom.

Peter concludes such individuals have forgotten their cleansing by the work of Christ. Having lost connection with the cross, they ultimately grow increasingly disconnected from God. Peter's warning is clear to all who will listen. They must turn from sin and pursue Christ. Spiritual growth is no option. It is a divine imperative.

Joyful, Yet Painful

For believers, the greatest joy comes when they sense that they are increasingly becoming formed into the character of Jesus their Lord. While all other forms of happiness are dependent upon circumstances, the joy that comes as a result of becoming who God intends them to be is wholly unique. It is a truly untouchable joy.

Like many other believers, while I possessed a deep desire to please the Lord, I found myself struggling with and at times overcome with the desires of my old nature. My first couple of years were often uneven in the sense that I possessed a deep commitment to Christ while at the same time continuing to lack an equal confidence that I would in the end remain faithful to the God I had come to increasingly love. I often asked myself, "Will I still be living for Jesus six months or a year from now?"

My initial three years or so were immensely paradoxical in this regard. On the one hand, the Holy Spirit through the people of Chestnut Assembly had given me a confidence I had never before experienced, yet on the other, I was plagued by a lack of confidence in my own strength to endure in my new faith. While a lack of confidence is undoubtedly a common dilemma for new believers, for me it would be a challenge to overcome. I had not been blessed with nurturing parents that instilled in me tools to deal with such challenges. God however knew my need and progressively provided what was needed. I like to say, "Although our pasts do not often provide many of the pieces necessary for our ultimate wholeness, we have a Father in heaven who has all those pieces that are missing." He will provide all we need as we trust and rest in Him.

Little by little and piece by piece, the Lord was giving me the things necessary for my spiritual formation. Without question, there were repeated times when I doubted that I would remain true to my early devotion, but God was providing me a track history. I was learning day by day that "He who began a good work in [me] will carry it on to completion" (Philippians 1:6).

The Call to Vocational Ministry

As time went by, I progressively came to sense that I wanted to spend my life in a vocation that was entirely devoted to furthering God's work in this world. I had no idea what the precise nature of my own vocational call would be, but I deeply sensed that I wanted to spend all my time and energy to serve the cause of Christ. I began to wonder what I needed to do to prepare for this ever-growing desire and sought counsel from Pastor Harry, Dwight Colbaugh, and Roz Flower.

I wasn't alone among my new brothers and sisters in this regard. A significant number of those who came to Jesus in the early years at Chestnut possessed similar desires. For two of us however, Steve Espamer and I, that call would ultimately lead us away from our treasured church to pursue the education and training necessary. Somehow we settled on a relatively small Assemblies of God school called Central Bible College in Springfield, Missouri, about 1,200 miles or so away. In the spring of 1973, we began to make plans to attend.

It is incredible to me how the Lord orders our lives sequentially. My high school grades and first semester at Cumberland County College were a complete disaster. But God helped me to miraculously develop some study skills that enabled me to graduate with a B+ grade point average. I left Cumberland County College with an associate degree in education and had largely repaired the educational deficit of my high school years. In the late spring of 1973, I received notice that I had been accepted for admission to CBC (Central Bible College).

Notwithstanding my acceptance, I faced the new challenge of financial provision. Although I received generous financial aid from the government, enough to pay for nearly all of my tuition and room and board, I would have no help from my financially strapped mom. I had to get a job during the summer of '73 in order to have the provisions necessary for my first semester of on-campus living. This need would lead to an incredible experience during that summer.

Grandma Salter's Grim Diagnosis

All of us at some time or another face the inevitable loss of loved ones. It was early in 1973, that Mom, Alice, and I received the news that Grandma Salter had been diagnosed with colon-rectal cancer. The three of us made the immediate decision to invite her to live with us, an invitation she initially refused. By early summer, her condition deteriorated to the point that it became necessary for her to receive better care. Ultimately she acquiesced to live with us.

Grandma Salter's living with us provided new opportunities for Alice and me to both verbally share the gospel with her and live out our faith in front of her. In the months that followed we began slowly but surely to notice a softening in her attitude. At first she would literally spit on the floor when we mentioned church or Jesus. After a while however, her hostility diminished somewhat and she seemed to become resigned to our life choices. Her illness and fears about death seemed to demand more of her emotional energy.

I refocused my gospel emphasis to stress the promise of eternal life to those who love Jesus and give their lives to Him. Although outwardly I saw no significant evidence that the message was getting through, I received great comfort and assurance as I prayed. Grandma Salter's eternal destiny would ultimately be in God's hands, and I instinctively knew that I would have to leave it with Him. I was determined to trust the Lord not only for my grandmother and mother, but also for my future. Despite my grandmother's illness, I felt peace about my decision to go to Bible college in the fall.

The Fine Line between Faith and Stupidity

There is often a fine line between responding in faith and doing really stupid things. Finding a summer job before leaving for Central Bible College was critical, and I aggressively searched all available options. Unfortunately for me, the economy was entering a slowdown and jobs were scarce. Although I had applications seemingly everywhere, I was coming up empty. By the middle of May, I was getting desperate.

My situation appeared to change when I saw an advertisement from Two Guys department stores detailing numerous openings in their local stores. Two Guys was a store chain that would be very similar to today's Walmart Supercenters. The stores had a department store section along with food sections that included a full line of meat, produce, and dairy, along with all other grocery items. I drove up in my sister's car to apply. As I entered the parking lot, I noticed that there were many people who were demonstrating against the store chain. As it turned out, they were Two Guys' employees who were on strike.

In the summer of 1973, I was a totally naïve twenty-one-year-old who urgently needed a job. I had no inkling of the hatred union members had for those who took their jobs while they were striking for better wages and benefits. As I drove through the parking lot, some people were cursing at me and I had no idea why. My mind was consumed with my immediate need to work and I assumed that the job was a provision of God. After the interview, I was hired to work in the produce department and was asked if I could start immediately. The words "start immediately" were music to my ears.

For all I knew the union could be on strike for the entire summer, so I was excited to begin. That people cursed at me every morning when I arrived was of little concern to me. I had a job and could make money to prepare for my full-time vocational calling. Nothing could deter me from receiving this "provision of God" for my life.

Unfortunately, the union strike against Two Guys department stores did not last the entire summer. In fact, it lasted only a little over a week. The second Monday following my hire the replacement workers received word that the union had settled and was set to approve a new labor contract. The department store was legally prohibited from letting replacement workers go after strikers returned to work. This was seldom if ever a problem because these workers never stayed around anyway, fearing retribution from returning employees. Such was the case of those who were temporary hires at Two Guys. Within two days all the replacement workers quit, that is all the replacement workers except one—me. I decided that I would ride it out. I could do so because I reasoned that God was my protector.

It is important to restate the radical nature of my early commitment to Jesus. I was determined to stay and work at Two Guys for two reasons. First, I believed that the Lord had miraculously provided the job. Secondly, I determined that running like everyone else was an act of unbelief. I reasoned that either God could protect me or He couldn't. My belief was that this was another in a seemingly long list of tests of my faith, and God had never failed me before.

On the day when regular employees returned to work, I began to receive threats to leave "if I knew what was good for me." The threats came from direct and indirect sources. Notes were left at my workstation and hostile comments were made within my hearing. When that didn't work, there were other attempts at intimidation. On multiple occasions, I would arrive at work to find produce all over the floor for me to pick up. Often I would have to wrap produce for display two or three times because I would find the packaged products unwrapped and on the floor. During all of this, I remained remarkably at peace. I deeply believed that the Lord would help me ride out the storm. My conviction was that somehow God would be glorified in what was taking place.

The situation reached a climax early one afternoon just days after the union workers returned. I was wrapping green bell peppers onto a Styrofoam plate with clear plastic as I did with most produce for display when I heard noise behind me. I turned to see a dozen or more employees from throughout the store gathered around me. Standing in front of them was a man named Bob. Bob, who was both the manager of the produce department and the union shop steward representing employees at the store, had a large slicing knife in his hand. With the men behind him watching, he proceeded to tell me that I needed to quit my job and leave the store immediately. With the supernatural help of the Holy Spirit, I calmly responded that I would not quit and was determined to remain at my job. At that moment, Bob pressed the knife against my diaphragm and told me that I had no choice. The union would simply not accept a "scab" (the common union term for replacement worker) to keep working at the store.

At that point I remember feeling something inside of me that defied the circumstances that surrounded me. I stared at Bob and said something to the effect that I was called into ministry and this job was provided to me by God to enable me to go to a Bible college. I told them they could do whatever they wanted to me but I was not leaving until the end of the summer. The men who had gathered were stunned at my response, and looked at each other not knowing what to say or do next. The next thing I remember was Bob telling the men who stood around me to go back to work. That was the last I heard of the matter for the entire summer.

To this day, I do not know how to characterize my stubborn refusal to leave Two Guys department store. Was it an act of faith or stupidity? The difference is often in the eye of the beholder. I do know however that the event was another building block in my growing confidence in God. Whether my actions were foolish or not, the Lord again showed himself able to intervene on my behalf.

During that summer at Two Guys department store another amazing thing took place. Bob, my produce manager and union shop steward, began to ask me questions about God. He said that he knew other new Christians including a friend of mine named Andy Robinson who had come to Christ shortly after I did and also attended Chestnut Assembly. Andy was a former drug user who had come to the Lord after a life crisis similar to mine. Bob was struck by both of our stories. In the weeks that followed, I was able to help him through a tough time in his marriage. While Bob did not commit his life to Christ during that summer, he experienced a softening to the gospel that was obvious. I don't know what came of Bob after I left in late August 1973, but I know that he was an important reason for my employment there.

Off to Bible College and Another Life Transition

My heart was both heavy and at peace when Steve Espamer and I left for Central Bible College late in the summer of 1973. I placed Grandma Salter and my family in God's hands and left for school not knowing what to expect. Springfield, Missouri, where the school was located was a 1,200 mile journey that took us approximately twenty-four hours by car. We left with a girl who was going to attend Evangel College (now Evangel University), an Assemblies of God liberal arts college in the same city. The three of us loaded up Steve's green 1967 Volkswagen Beetle to the absolute max. Most of the stuff was Steve's (he had all sorts of things he thought he needed.) I basically left for school with one small trunk of possessions. His stuff filled half of the car trunk along with part of the back seat and things tied to the car's roof. As we passed through the mountains of Pennsylvania, at times we doubted the VW would make it, but it did.

I remember arriving on campus in awe of what this new chapter of my life would bring. The campus was small and a mix of old and newer buildings. Steve and I had decided to room together. About a week before classes were to start, we got room keys for our new home located in Welch Hall, third floor west. My life had come far since that October afternoon in 1970. A little less than three years had gone by and many incredible things had happened in such a short period of time. As I reflected back on the past two years and ten-and-a-half months, I recognized that I had grown spiritually in so many ways. Fears were undoubtedly still there, but they were clearly receding. My confidence in both God and myself was increasing, and a new Michael Jaffe was being formed.

Chapter 16
Loving God with My Mind

"Hearing that Jesus had silenced the Sadducees, the Pharisees got together. One of them, an expert in the law, tested him with this question: 'Teacher, which is the greatest commandment in the Law?'
Jesus replied: 'Love the Lord your God with all your heart and with all your soul and with all your mind. *This is the first and greatest commandment. And the second is like it: 'Love your neighbor as yourself.' All the Law and the Prophets hand on these two commandments.' "*
Matthew 22:34-40 (my emphasis)

"If we are going to be wise, spiritual people prepared to meet the crises of our age, we must be a studying, learning community that values the life of the mind."
—J.P. Moreland

The United Negro College Fund used to run an advertisement that featured the slogan, "A mind is a terrible thing to waste." The slogan, I believe can apply to the Christian's approach to God. Often believers fail to appreciate the role of the mind in understanding God. In other words, spirituality is consistent with an ability to think. God created our brains and fully intends that we use them in our pursuit of Him.

The Great Commandment instructs us to love the Lord our God with all our heart, soul, and mind. In commanding us to do so, Jesus emphasizes the need to employ our entire beings in our devotion to the Lord. Our rational processes are as spiritual as the emotional aspects of who we are. We are called upon to think as well as feel.

I have always been a "left-brained" sort of person. Reason and rationality are important to my ability to apprehend God with any level of confidence. Things must make sense to me. They need to be reasonable. Just because I wanted something to be true did not mean that it was true in fact.

I am convinced that God does not want us to place our brains on a shelf and be led about solely by our emotions and desires. Faith is not separate from reason. It is and must be eminently reasonable. If Christianity is true, then it must make sense. The Christian faith is not blind faith. It is the most reasonable explanation for life as we know it.

It has always been crucial for me to be convinced that I did not merely believe in Jesus Christ simply because I needed to believe. My life had been a painful one. The healing balm of a loving God who knew who I was turned out to be beyond welcome. He had given me peace and hope for the future, but that did not make Jesus the true Son of God. The reality of who Jesus is had to be built upon something much more secure or I never could have been satisfied.

An Audacious Faith

You have undoubtedly heard the question often: How can you say that Jesus is the only way to God? This question presents believers with quite a challenge. Can we say with confidence that our religion is right and all others wrong, or at the least lacking a complete understanding of truth? Are there objective and rational reasons to believe that Jesus and Jesus alone is the way to eternal life?

Most people think it is utterly audacious for Christians to believe that they possess the only complete truth. For a short time my dramatic life-changing experience was enough to sustain my faith. Before long however, I found myself desiring more. True, I sensed the Spirit of God within me. Clearly there was a sense of peace and meaning to life that I had not previously known. There was also the testimony of friends and others I had come to know who had partaken of the same Jesus with the same apparent life transformations. But could my faith meet the tests of reason? I simply had to be convinced.

The environment of Central Bible College was a timely greenhouse for my pursuit of a faith that was defendable and satisfying. An opportunity was available for me to ask questions and receive answers. My first semester during the fall of 1973 marked the beginning of what would turn out to be an important new chapter in my faith development.

Godly Professors and Sounding Boards

I was about to learn that the mind had a lot to do with a Christian's faith. Up to this point, I had been feeding off the energy of encounters with God and the new sense of personal confidence poured into me by others. My instincts told me that these experiences would not be enough to sustain a lifelong commitment. I was less than three years removed from my previous life of uncertainty and aimlessness. While these three years or so represented the longest sustained period of commitment to anything, I could not escape the question, "Will I still be following this path two, five or ten years in the future?"

One of the first things I remember doing after I got settled on campus was to look over the college catalogue. Of particular interest to me was the section that detailed the academic credentials of the faculty. Who, after all, were the faculty members that would have opportunity to shape my life in the next few years? I wanted to know that they could be trusted academically and spiritually.

During the early years of my Christian life, I had wonderful mentors from whom I could draw. Pastor Harry, Dwight, and Roz who made up the pastoral staff and the wonderful people of Chestnut Assembly were deeply influential and taught me incredible things. I couldn't have hoped for a godlier group of people to lead me into the varied dimensions of what it meant to follow Jesus. They laid a strong foundation, but I had additional questions and I eagerly anticipated relationships with faculty and students alike.

The faculty of Central Bible College at the time I had enrolled consisted of men and women who had graduate degrees either at the masters or doctoral level. In addition, they had a wealth of experience in various aspects of Christian ministry. Their degrees came from both well-regarded seminaries and universities. Because I came to CBC with an associate degree in education, most of my general education requirements had already been met. The courses that remained for my bachelor's degree were mostly in the fields of biblical and theological studies and practical ministry.

I could not wait for my first semester to begin. The thought of learning about the history of the Bible world and great beliefs of the Christian church was new and exhilarating. I would be sitting in classes of professors with PhDs who could impart understandings that I hadn't been able to receive. This excitement was augmented by the sense that God had led me to this place. God's hand was clearly on my life. I was exactly where He wanted me to be.

It soon became clear to me that not everyone who was a student at Central Bible College was as enamored with the moment in the same way I was. For a number of new students, the college experience seemed to be an opportunity to get away from home and the strict control of parents. It was not uncommon to witness classmates experimenting with spiritual compromise as a result of their new freedom. But there were also large numbers of students who possessed the same desire to learn about God as I did. I made it a point to cultivate relationships with those I could share and make new intellectual and spiritual discoveries with.

Whether in the classroom or the dormitory, it seemed that for me theological discussions were the norm not the exception. I loved challenging others with my thoughts and being challenged by theirs. At first, it was a little difficult to value the strongly held views of those whose opinions differed significantly from my own. It was in effect a lesson in humility to grasp that beliefs held by classmates were potentially valid even though I disagreed with them strongly. I was learning that an academic environment was meant to provide opportunities for intellectual give-and-take.

Two Steps Forward and One Step Back

My first semester was a time of growth at many different levels, but it was not all "onward and upward." Central Bible College in the early 1970s was, by most standards, a reasonably strict institution when it came to behavioral standards. Students had midnight curfews on weeknights, and these curfews were only relaxed slightly on Friday and Saturday evenings to 1 a.m. While jeans were allowed generally on campus, they were not accepted in the classroom or in daily chapels. Hair was not allowed over the ears for male students and neither was facial hair with the exceptions of mustaches, which could be no lower than the corner of the lip. Attending movies, along with a number of other activities were expressly forbidden and, to make matters worse, keeping one's room clean was required as was making one's bed.

It should not be a surprise to anyone that these restrictions were a struggle for me. I had been my own master since I was thirteen years old and thought that these lifestyle decisions were beneath a person of my background. Externally, I submitted but internally I resented the interference into my autonomy. I remember becoming extremely angry on one occasion when my dorm counselor reprimanded me for failing a random bed check. I was able to tolerate such indignities only because the Lord had given me a deep sense that this was God's place for me. I also deeply loved the things I was learning. But seeds of a critical spirit were beginning to form that would periodically hamper my spiritual growth.

The truth is spiritual growth is almost never a straight, inclining upward line. It is more like the jagged line of the Dow Jones Industrial Average of the New York Stock Exchange. Just as God was effecting rapid spiritual growth in my life, I was simultaneously experiencing setbacks. I was growing and struggling at the same time.

The pattern ultimately continued throughout my college experience. Periods of cynicism however were more times than not overpowered by a deep and increasing theological formation. Many people fail to grasp the role theology can play in their spiritual formation. The term *theology* essentially comes from two Greek roots *theos* (God) and *logos* (reasoning or study). It refers to the study of God.

Christianity teaches that God desires a relationship with His creation, and Jesus died to make that relationship possible. As in any meaningful bond between persons, it is required that those involved know who one another are. The problem is not on God's end. He knows us completely, but we often fail to know and understand Him. Any false or skewed knowledge will adversely impact the quality of the relationship.

Christian theology reveals what the Scriptures teach concerning the nature, character, and attributes of God. It tells us that God is loving, merciful, compassionate, and faithful, but also holy, righteous, and just. The more we apprehend the Lord through His revelation, the more we can worship Him in Spirit and truth. Adequate theological understanding leads to a wholesome spiritual formation.

I remember a specific occasion when a more complete understanding of what Jesus did for me on the cross transformed my walk with God. It occurred in a theology class. One of my professors was lecturing on what he called "the finished work of Christ." As a part of the lecture he examined the theological meaning of justification. He stated that as a result of Jesus' atoning death for our sins, believers are placed "in Christ" and are seen by the Lord as clothed in His righteousness. The night prior to the lecture I had failed God in a way that caused me to doubt my standing with Him. My professor's words enabled me to not only feel released from the guilt and condemnation I was experiencing, but to also recognize that my standing with the Lord was dependent on my faith in what Jesus achieved on my behalf and not on any momentary failure. I became free to love God from a place of confidence rather than fear.

The Passing of Grandma Salter

My first semester seemed to pass by in a flash. In a few short months I had made a number of friends, developed nurturing relationships with professors, and, most of all, began to cultivate a relationship with God that was broader and deeper than I thought possible. What was most incredible to me however was the ever-growing sense of the Lord's hand on my life.

Just two days before the end of my initial semester however, I received news that Grandma Salter was near death. The news was not a shock in the sense that I knew her cancer would likely take her life before too long. My concern was for her eternal salvation and I prayed for one more opportunity to share with her that Jesus loved her and had died in order to enable her to live with Him for all eternity. I completed my exams and caught the first flight home I could get. When I arrived it was too late. Grandma Salter died while I was in the air.

What I did not know was the Lord was working in ways I could not imagine. Alice recounted to me the full story of His miraculous working in my grandmother's life. While at school I had become aware of the fact Grandma Salter's physical situation had been gradually deteriorating. During that time, she had to be placed in a nursing facility and she knew that her time was limited. Grandma, like Mom, feared death in ways that I believe were greater than most.

My eighty-one-year-old grandmother was placed in a double room with an elderly woman who I believe had severe dementia. The woman's son was Don Breeden who was one of the people in Chestnut Assembly who had significantly impacted my first couple of years after coming to faith. He was an extraordinarily compassionate man who literally oozed the love of Jesus. During his visits to see his mother, Don gradually engaged Grandma Salter in general conversations not knowing that she was our grandmother.

One day Alice and Mom arrived at the nursing facility only to find Don talking to Grandma Salter. Alice was astonished to learn that Don's mother was Grandma's roommate, and Don was equally astonished to find out that the woman he had been conversing with was our grandmother. Needless to say, that caused him to redouble his efforts to express the love of Jesus to her. Don became her almost-daily visitor, sometimes reading the Bible to her and on other occasions singing comforting hymns. She came to treasure his visits.

We often underestimate how valuable it is to be with people during the most critical times of life. When my grandmother was facing her greatest fears, Don Breeden was there to love her and lead her through to the end of life. He was God's provision and angel of mercy that led her to eternity. During Grandma Salter's final hours, Don and Pastor Harry from Chestnut Assembly led her to a profession of faith. To this very day, I am in awe of the way God worked in my family, more of which I will share in later chapters.

Grandma Salter's passing led to one awkward experience that reminded me of our still very strained family relations. Members of my extended family from Philadelphia came to my grandmother's graveside service. It was a Jewish burial performed by a rabbi that I did not know. My only recollection of the service is that no one in the family spoke a word to Alice and me. The estrangement between us and most of our extended family has remained to this day.

A New Close Friend

When I returned to school in January of 1974 for the spring semester, I again arrived with anticipation. Steve and I planned to room together again, and we excitedly returned to Welch Hall to resume our educational journey. When we entered the lobby in Welch, we noticed a tall, slender student playing his guitar. Steve and I immediately introduced ourselves. He was arriving late and as a result didn't have an assigned room. The three of us hit it off immediately, and we applied to the school for a suite that could accommodate more than two students. As fortune would have it, the students who previously lived in one of the suites on the first floor split up and needed smaller accommodations. Alan Mallory became our new roommate and close friend.

It is hard to overstate how much Alan meant to my personal and spiritual growth during the final two-and-a-half years of my Central Bible College experience. Alan was from the tiny town of Mullen, which is located in the Nebraska Sand Hills. He couldn't have been outwardly more different than Steve and me. We were from New Jersey and Alan, at least to us, couldn't have been more hillbilly. In addition to guitar, he played the banjo, the mandolin, and a mean harmonica. It seemed as though every night was a jam session with Steve, Alan, and others who would happen by.

Because I had no car during my first year-and-a-half at school, Alan's Oldsmobile 88 was my typical means of transportation. He generally took me wherever I needed to go. In addition to my constant need for transportation, I was almost always broke. Even though I worked on campus, most of my earnings went toward my tuition or room and board. When Alan and I went out for food which was often since neither of us could stand the college cuisine, he nearly always bought my food. I would jokingly tell him that when doing his income taxes, he should declare me as a dependent.

I tried to repay Alan's generosity by helping him through difficult personal struggles. For hours on end, I encouraged him in a number of areas of his life. When all was said and done, we were great for each other, each helping the other at his greatest perceived point of need.

Perhaps the best part of our friendship was the stimulating

theological discussions that took place on a regular basis. We took a number of the same classes because our major was biblical studies. Both of us loved the Scriptures and we loved learning about God. Our conversations influenced us and developed us spiritually more than we probably realized at the time. Decades later, I still regard Alan as one of the closest friends I ever had.

The Formation of a Spiritual Identity

I regard my three years at Central Bible College as the years that most significantly established my Christian identity. It was during that time that my mind experienced the greatest transformation. I came to understand who I was in Christ.

It is still my strong belief that a deep Christian spiritual identity is an extremely powerful tool in a person's spiritual formation. The Bible over and over reminds us who we are in God's eyes. We are children of God, dearly loved, elect, regenerated by the Holy Spirit and righteous through the blood of Jesus. We are a chosen race, a royal priesthood, a holy nation, and a people who are called God's very possession (1 Peter 2:9) for the purpose of bringing Him eternal glory.

It was my years at Central Bible College that taught me the value of my mind. I would have more educational experiences in the years to come, but none would be more impacting. There would need to be more healing to come in my life. I was learning rapidly however that the Lord could be counted upon to bring about this healing one stage at a time, and the healing would begin with the renewing of my mind.

Chapter 17
My Greatest Earthly Treasure

"The LORD *God said, 'It is not good for the man to be alone. I will make a helper suitable for him.'"*
—Genesis 2:18

"He who finds a wife finds what is good and receives favor from the LORD.*"*
—Proverbs 18:22

"A wife of noble character who can find?
She is worth far more than rubies.
Her husband has full confidence in her
and lacks nothing of value.
She brings him good, not harm, all the days of her life."
—Proverbs 31:10–12

Spiritual growth is much more complicated than a person typically thinks. Just when you think you are making real progress, you become aware of new areas in your life that await your attention. Often the areas that need attention are not in the realms that are normally considered within the domain of the spiritual. The truth is everything in the believer's life is in the domain of the spiritual.

Unfortunately for me, I had atrophied socially when it

came to my confidence level with members of the opposite sex. There were a number of reasons for this, but mainly it was because I had little experience with girls who came from Christian backgrounds. I sometimes felt out of place in their company, not knowing how to act. The things with which they were familiar were largely foreign to me.

For the most part, these awkward feelings kept me from dating girls during my first year at college. While I was outgoing in some respects, I was not outgoing around girls. Among my friends, Steve seemed to have the most confidence when it came to our female classmates. I envied his ability to risk asking girls out even though he was on occasion rejected. My ability to withstand rejection by the opposite sex was much more limited.

A Strange Dare Reaps an Unexpected Payoff

Everything changed in a hurry for me late in the fall of 1974. A friend of mine named Tom and I were encouraging Alan to pursue either of two girls he had expressed interest in. He said that he couldn't make up his mind between the two and resolved to do nothing until he did. Alan was an extremely laid-back individual probably due to his rural "sand hills" background. He was never in a hurry and always maintained that he had plenty of time to do whatever was before him. His laid-back attitude was a big joke among all his friends.

Weeks went by and Alan still found himself unable to choose between the two potential girlfriends. Day after day we would try to encourage him to act, but he refused. Finally in desperation, Tom and I threatened to ask them out if he wouldn't. I think Tom and I were each deep down interested in the girls, Tom in one and me the other. Alan determined to call our bluff and challenged us to go ahead if we wanted to. (We did and within two years both of us ended up marrying the girl we had been interested in.)

As it turned out, Tom and I were really more interested in the two girls than was Alan. I must confess however, that Alan was not in the least jealous of either of us. In fact, he cheered us on and was thoroughly happy for us. Because I was genuinely afraid to ask the girl out that I was interested in, Alan even offered to help. We decided to both ask her to go to an event. It was a comical sight to say the least. We both met her in the dorm lobby. The girl sat between us in the front seat of Alan's Oldsmobile. When the evening was over, we both walked her back to the dorm. Afterward, when asked by her roommate who her date was, she replied astonishingly, "I really don't know."

It wasn't long before Barbara Taseff would find out that I was the one who was interested in getting to know her. My timidity would continue for the next couple of weeks or so, but increasingly I would seek her out in the dining commons or elsewhere on campus, and it became more and more clear to her that I was the one who was at least somewhat interested. The difficult thing for me was transitioning into an actual dating relationship. This all seemed new to me because I was totally out of practice.

As Christmas approached I felt like I had to make my intentions more clear. I procrastinated as long as possible but time was running out before the semester break, and leaving for the holidays with the situation unclear would have been frustrating. I soon came to understand that God was interested in all the areas of my life, not just my devotional life and call to vocational ministry. It is amazing to me how easy it is to relegate the Lord to the so-called "spiritual" parts of life and convince ourselves that our other concerns are outside

His interest. I prayed and asked Him to help me to get my message across without being overly foolish.

I didn't have much money so I settled on a single pink carnation. My plan was to call and ask her to meet me because I had something to give her. There I stood in my navy blue winter coat with the single carnation in hand. I vividly remember how embarrassingly stupid I felt. My most important question however, was, how would she react? I convinced myself that I would know by the look on her face as she approached. As I saw her from a distance, her warm smile was evident and I knew all was well. Deep within, I was thanking God for His help and learning that He cared about the real stuff of life.

My confidence was clearly on the increase as I made my way back to the dorm. I remember asking Alan if I should call her during Christmas break. I was afraid of coming on too strong, yet I wanted Barbara to know that I was really interested. He encouraged me to call her, but I went back and forth in my mind. Whether or not to call her occupied my thinking the entire Christmas break. To call or not to call, that was the question. After much prayer, I took a chance and called Christmas afternoon. I will never forget her words, "I don't believe you!" Again I had made a good impression and knew that God was helping me. What an incredible thing, I thought. The Creator of the universe cares about everything in my life!

First Comes Love, Then Comes Marriage

Finding the person God has for you is an incredible thing for anyone, but as far as I was concerned, the reality left me with a deep sense of awe. A part of my baggage from the past was the lingering sense that the basic elements of a life of happiness were for others but not me. Because there is no delete button that automatically erases negative thoughts and feelings from our pasts, we are often burdened with many attitudes that are self-demeaning and seriously harmful. We have to learn that God is both able and willing to restore and bless us.

Meeting Barb without question was the greatest single reality affirming this truth to my heart. Loving parents give gifts and my loving Heavenly Father was in the midst of giving me the most meaningful gift in my earthly life. At the time, I was preoccupied with all the things that accompany falling in love. Little did I realize then how much loving and being loved would accelerate my inner healing.

Relationships can mature quickly on a college campus. Each day we ate lunch and dinner together. This was a real transition since prior to my meeting Barb, I would eat with a variety of people. Once we started dating, that all changed. The two of us spent virtually every moment possible together during the spring semester of 1975. During spring break I went to her home in northwest Indiana to meet her family, and as we returned to school afterward, I was certain that we were meant to be.

My proposal came in May of that year (I know that seems quick, but these things can happen rapidly in a Bible college environment). I arranged to go home with her after the end of the spring semester to pop the question. I proposed at Indiana Dunes Park next to a tree during a picnic. She accepted. That evening we broke the news to her parents and it was announced to the entire family. As it turned out, no one was surprised, which baffled me some. I didn't think that I was that obvious.

The summer of 1975 was difficult for us in one significant respect. Barb and I wouldn't see each other from May until the end of August. We went our separate ways, each fulfilling a requirement for graduation that involved a summer ministry internship. Barb had committed to serve at a Teen Challenge in Phoenix, Arizona, while I had been accepted to do an internship at Leavenworth Federal Penitentiary in Leavenworth, Kansas.

(Before I go on perhaps a word of explanation is in order. When I arrived at Central Bible College in the fall of 1973, I almost immediately became involved at the United States Medical Center for Federal Prisoners, also located in Springfield, Missouri. I ministered to inmates in the hospital wards, taught Bible studies, attended church services there, and eventually became the leader of the ministry that included approximately a dozen students. It actually became my home church while at college. During my three years at CBC, I became convinced that the Lord was calling me to be a chaplain in the Federal Bureau of Prisons. The chaplain at the Fed Med, as we called it, was very encouraging and appreciated the ministry conducted by the students from our college.)

The summer of separation was difficult for Barb and me, but we wrote to each other every day. Barb has saved all those letters, but I refuse to read them. They are too embarrassingly representative of a poor, lovesick boy. We eventually made it through the summer and had a glorious reuniting before our final school year.

Barb and I were married on May 29,1976, in Merrillville, Indiana. On that day, I inherited a wonderful family that would supply a deep sense of familial identity. Barb's family was and still is a very close, supportive, and loving community that has always known how to laugh, cry, and be together. Her mom, Olga, and dad, George, received me as part of the family instantaneously. Her sisters, Patty and Karen, and brother Bob, like their parents provided me with the kind of cohesive, nurturing environment in adulthood that I did not have as a child and teenager. Barb's extended family, especially her Aunt Alice and Uncle Alvin and Aunt Irene and Uncle Barney, always were a part of regular family gatherings that included an annual Thanksgiving get-together of thirty-five to forty family members. It has been said that when you marry a person you marry a family, and I could not be more thankful for that reality.

The First Few Years

Following our honeymoon, which was a low budget week in Bailey's Harbor, Wisconsin, we packed all of our meager belongings into the backseat and trunk of an orange 1970 Cadillac Sedan Deville and moved to Fort Worth, Texas, where I would complete a master of divinity degree at Southwestern Baptist Theological Seminary. I chose Southwestern Baptist for two reasons. First, it came highly recommended. Dwight Colbaugh, my first youth pastor, attended there and thought highly of the school. Second, I found out through Dwight that the seminary gave what were virtually full scholarships to all who were accepted. During the late 1970s, this applied to all students regardless of their denominational affiliation. I later heard that the Southern Baptists granted these scholarships to up to 5 percent of those who were accepted as students from outside the Southern Baptist Convention. All of their scholarship funds, I believe, came from what was called a Cooperative Program supplied through their churches. I gladly and gratefully accepted their generosity.

A master of divinity was required for those who pursued chaplaincy within the Federal Bureau of Prisons and initially that was my sense of calling. While I was completing my degree, Barb was also in school finishing her bachelor's degree in elementary education at Texas Christian University, also located in Fort Worth. Because we were newly married with a very limited income, Barb's family provided the money necessary for her to finish her bachelor's degree.

During most of the three years we spent there (1976–1979), we were both full-time students and worked as much as possible on the side in order to survive. Our income was extremely meager, but we were content to be just south of the poverty line. While I was used to being poor, Barb was not. Her family, although not rich by any means, provided for her well. Despite not being used to living hand to mouth, Barb was amazingly able to make the necessary adjustments. She seemed to make a seamless transition to the financial challenges we faced and never complained.

One Flesh and One Spirit

Genesis 2:24 declares, "That is why a man leaves his father and mother and is united to his wife, and they become one flesh." The apostle Paul in his letter to the church at Ephesus quotes the Genesis passage in his brief discourse concerning the relationship between husbands and wives. The passages emphasize the truth that God created men and women as complements to one another and established a mystical union intended to encompass the entirety of their beings. This union is far greater than a mere sexual union, but embraces a union that is both physical and spiritual.

When a man and a woman enter into this mystical union, it is God's intent that they experience its intended blessing. This, of course, is in a large sense dependent upon the individuals involved. It is the responsibility of the man and the woman to become able to bless and be blessed, love and be loved. Each individual retains the ability to fulfill God's intended purpose for their union. They, however, must supply the effort by practicing service. Each must determine to count the other as more important than self.

Without question, the greatest earthly blessing of my life is God's gift of Barb. By His grace and mercy, He gave me a person who is extraordinarily capable of giving and receiving love. Many times I would like to take credit for the choice I made. It would be easy to refer to myself as wise in my selection of a life partner. That would miss the point entirely. While there is an aspect to this that may be true in that we do possess the ability to make both good and bad choices, it was the Lord who placed my soul mate in my path and caused my heart to be smitten with her. It would turn out that no one would have a greater role in my spiritual and emotional growth and development.

Restorative Love

My wife's role in what became the rapid healing of my whole person is beyond question. I daresay that this truth is far beyond her own understanding. Generally speaking, people underestimate their power to affect others for good or for bad. In a marriage, this is especially true.

The initial half-a-dozen years of my life as a Christian were amazingly restorative on the one hand, yet at the same time they exposed wounds that lingered beneath the surface. I continued to struggle with a critical spirit along with identity and self-esteem issues. Some of these issues healed more rapidly than others, but much of the healing was the result of the unconditional and affirming love of the life partner given to me by God.

Later I would come to understand what was behind Barb's role in my healing process. While it is one thing to grasp

God's love in a theological or theoretical way, it is more difficult to experience it. The reason for this is that we have to unlearn so many things. For my part, Barb became the first human being who loved me for who I was and that gave me something from which I could tangibly derive value. When a person loves you in this way, a new sense of self-value and self-worth is able to begin to form. In short, I was deeply valued by Barb, and as a result came to realize that I had significance.

I occasionally wonder what my spiritual growth would have looked like if I had been married to someone else who was less committed to me. The two of us entered the relationship with the understanding that we were committed for life. We intuitively recognized the interconnectedness between our bond with Christ and each other. This understanding allowed for a maximum of benefit for both of us. Our relationship over time enhanced our confidence, faith, and wholeness.

When I look at the creation of the woman from the Genesis account (2:18, 20–25), I cannot help but appreciate its significance. Verse 18 declares, "The Lord God said, 'It is not good for the man to be alone. I will make a helper *suitable for him*' " (my emphasis). In wonder, I reflect upon His choice of a complement for me. While Barb is by no means a perfect person, she is and has always been perfect for me.

A Partner in Vocational Ministry

The three years at Southwestern Baptist Theological Seminary went by quickly. We made great friends who are still our friends today, although I must confess I have not kept in close contact with many. One of my weaknesses is that I allow this to happen. People like Jim and Kathy O'Dillon, Mike

Moseng, Dan and Deb Strickland, David Penley and others were a real part of my spiritual growth. On occasion I think of the times I spent with these wonderful people. The years spent in Fort Worth were a special part of our lives, partly I'm sure because it was the first years of our marriage.

As Barb and I approached graduation in our respective programs, it was time to look forward to the callings placed upon our lives. Although my initial sense was a call to chaplaincy within the United States Department of Corrections, over time I had come to feel that my giftings were more consistent with a teaching ministry. I felt especially directed to teach in the areas of biblical studies and theology. In response to this sense of direction, I applied to the colleges within my denomination (I had obtained ministry credentials with the Assemblies of God during my last year at seminary) and received the same reply from all of them. For someone desiring to teach in the fields of biblical studies and theology, a minimum of two years of pastoral experience was required.

Barb and I, after considerable prayer, decided to investigate ministry opportunities. Ultimately, we took a trip to New York to interview for two positions, one that was able to pay us a livable salary and one that was not. When the interviews were over, neither of us discussed our feelings until we were well on the way to the Newark Airport to return to Texas. My private sense was that God was calling us to the position that couldn't pay us a salary that could support us. I was resisting the feeling because in all honesty I was tired of being poor. After all the hard work of finishing my master of divinity, I wanted a change from the meager subsistence that had characterized my entire life, and the nudging of the Spirit was not exactly welcomed.

I was hoping Barb would say that the God was leading her in a different direction, but as you probably guessed, her feelings were the same as mine. We shared our feelings with one another and although we resolved to pray further about it, both of us were convinced of the call to Trinity Assembly of God in Middletown, New York, as youth and associate pastor.

In the years to come, our ministry at this wonderful church would become a rich blessing in a multitude of ways. From this experience, I learned something much more important. My life partner was willing to follow the Lord wherever He would lead us. She was not only a perfect partner in life, she would also be a perfect partner in my life calling.

Chapter 18
Blessed Fatherhood

"Children are a heritage from the LORD,
offspring a reward from him.
Like arrows in the hands of a warrior
are children born in one's youth.
Blessed is the man whose quiver is full of them.
They will not be put to shame when they contend
with their opponents in court."
—Psalm 127:3–5

When Barb and I mused about becoming parents, I told her that I desired to have three sons. It was not a prophetic understanding in any way, but it was a desire that I stated on more than one occasion. I would also joke about naming our first son Amos. Actually, I was serious about both (having a son and naming him Amos that is). When I mentioned this to Barb, she loved the idea of having three sons but there was no way she was going to name any of them Amos. That was totally out of the question.

In bringing up the matter of having children in general and sons in particular, there was much more behind it than Barb or even I realized. The desire to have sons was rooted in something deep within my psyche. I didn't grasp it at the time, but when the day arrived feelings I didn't know I was capable of manifested themselves. Only much later did I come to understand why fatherhood would be so important to my sense of significance.

The Middletown Church

Trinity Assembly of God in Middletown, New York, was a blessing to our lives in so many ways. There we had friends, a loving congregation, a meaningful ministry, and just about everything else imaginable, except money of course. But as it turned out, any lack of material means was overwhelmed by the blessing of being in the will of God. The church gave us so much more than we gave them. The friends and wonderful memories of the five years we spent there are still with us.

The pastor was Jerry Bricker. I could go on and on about the things this man taught me, most of which came from watching how he lived and cared for those to whom he ministered. From Jerry, I learned not only how to practice ministry but more importantly what it meant to be a spiritual man. I treasured the conversations we had when we drove together to special events. Jerry and his wife Jeanne were special gifts to Barb and me.

From the first weeks, I was given the opportunity to develop my preaching skills. Jerry proposed a schedule where he would preach in the Sunday morning service and I would preach in the evening. There was no question in my mind that he was fully invested in my personal and professional development. In time, I was given the opportunity to preach occasionally in the Sunday morning services as well, as the two of us became partners in ministry.

About two years into my time of ministry in Middletown, the congregation entered into a building program that nearly tripled the attendance at Trinity. Eventually, my salary increased as the church grew. Our entire experience there was nothing but positive and fulfilling. When I reflect back, I often wonder what it would have been like if I had chosen a different place to begin ministry, one that could have paid me more but not provide the positive experience that I could carry with me through the rest of my life.

The Stunning Announcement

Three years into our ministry in Middletown and six years into our marriage, Barb announced to me that she was pregnant. My response was a mixture of joy and disbelief. Actually, it might be more accurate to describe it as a mixture of joy and unbelief. While the joy is easily understandable, the disbelief or unbelief needs to be explained.

My difficulty in believing either my wife or the doctor for that matter had a great deal to do with the tragic death of my father when I was barely a teenager. Deep within my subconscious self, I felt somehow unworthy of the privilege and joy of fatherhood. I know this makes no sense to anyone with a mature view of the nature and character of God. The truth is however people typically struggle with feelings that make no sense but are inextricably linked to past experiences. The shame I felt over my father's suicide was unfair and unnecessary, but all too real nonetheless. It took many years for me to fully recover from this traumatic event. In fact, it is difficult to know what vestiges remain even to this day.

Barb's first pregnancy and the birth of our first child would in many ways prove to be a watershed experience in this regard. It was only in about the fourth month of the pregnancy when I was away from home on a trip with the church youth group that I began to have confidence that it was all true. Ironically, I was taking some of our teenagers to Springfield, Missouri, to visit our two Assemblies of God colleges,

Central Bible College and Evangel College. Barb called to say that she had heard the heartbeat. Somehow at that point, it dawned on me that I was really going to be a father.

There was no question in my mind that our child would be a boy. We decided to name him Joshua (I had given up on naming him Amos). Barb and I both loved the name Joshua so there was no disagreement whatsoever. In the near-impossible event that it would be a girl, we had a few girls' names in reserve.

As the due date drew near, we spent many evenings feeling for Josh's movement. We counted the days, which seemed to make the months go by exceedingly slowly. When we were about a month from the due date, we enrolled in birthing classes. I was surprised and excited to learn that I would be allowed in the birthing room, since I was used to the movies depicting men waiting in another room for the doctor or nurse to come in and announce the birth and gender of the baby. Even more amazing to me was the news that I would not only be there to witness the delivery but also to be a valued part of the experience. Despite every evidence to the contrary, deep down there was still an abiding fear within me that something would prevent this experience from actually taking place.

He Arrives

It was on an Easter Sunday afternoon when Barb announced that she thought she was in labor. We called Pastor Jerry to apprise him of the situation and left for Horton Hospital late in the afternoon once we were sure that the labor had begun. When we arrived and had Barb checked out, the attending nurse determined that we had jumped the gun because labor was still in its very early stages. Nonetheless we were allowed to stay while nurses monitored the situation.

Hours went by and there was little progress. After another examination, the nurse came to the same conclusion she had previously that Barb was in labor but her progress was slow. Her diagnosis was that Barb was still in the early to middle stages. The nurse offered us the opportunity to go home and wait, but we were too nervous and declined. In retrospect, I think the only reason she even gave us the option was because she sensed our apprehension and felt she could let us stay because beds were available.

Then it happened; severe labor pains arrived. After nearly eighteen hours of "nothing labor," the contractions came on like gangbusters. In what seemed to be no time, Joshua was born. He not only had a very full head of black hair, he had hair on his forehead. Joshua was a unique looking child in that regard, but most important of all was the truth that he was mine or I guess I should say ours.

What an incredibly joyous experience! I never felt as euphoric as I did that day during his birth. I would spend a lot of my time watching him in the nursery and bursting with pride when people would look in and exclaim. "Look at that hairy baby!" I was a real father. I had a son of my own.

Becoming vs. Being

Kent Nerburn was once quoted as saying, "It is much easier to become a father than to be one." During the next thirty-three years, I would learn firsthand the truth of that statement. As it turned out, Josh would be the first of three children Barb and I would be blessed with, and each would present his own respective challenges and special joys.

Our firstborn was a challenge to get to sleep, and we were

nervous when he cried for long periods before succumbing to sleep for the night. We would take turns getting up to rock him to sleep, often with limited success. But we had all the energy of youth and endured the challenge. All the inconveniences aside, for me there was nothing like being a father. If I had accomplished little else in life, that in itself would be enough to provide me with significant meaning.

That being said, there were times that I felt incredibly inadequate. My recollections of my own father were far too few for me to have much to draw from in terms of modeling. I would have to learn on the fly and trust the Lord for the knowledge and wisdom necessary. One thing I did know, however; I wanted to provide a thousand times more than I had received as a child. I was determined to provide all the guidance, love, and friendship to Josh that I was deprived of after my own dad's untimely passing.

I would learn that fatherhood requires incredible sacrifice, patience, humility, and persistence. It requires the overcoming of a man's greatest nemesis—selfishness. A father has to often sacrifice his own desires and pursuits in order to pour self-esteem and self-worth into his children. Without this sacrifice, children will grow up with serious handicaps when it comes to their sense of self. Fatherhood is both an awesome privilege and a lot of hard work.

But, of course, being a father is an amazingly fulfilling experience. Nothing is more special than the joy felt when your child runs up to you with his arms wide open as you come home from work. Nothing is more special than the look in your child's eyes that exclaim, "You are the most important person in the world." Fatherhood opens up a world of new possible joyful experiences that are rooted in loving and serving. It changes your entire life perspective. And one more thing . . . it adds to your sense of value. When a child demonstrates how important you are to him, you realize how vital you become to a person who needs you for so many reasons.

Your first child is unique because, well, he or she is your first. Every stage of the child's growth and development is a new experience. When your son recognizes you for the first time, it is a wonderful thrill. The first time he attempts to communicate and the first time he sits up on his own become huge deals. Then comes the child's first locomotion, his first steps, and his first words. You can't wait for all the milestones. They are beyond special.

As Josh was growing, I found myself enthralled in the wonderful new sensation of becoming a father. But it would become a real learning experience as well. There were times when I would wish that I had more pictures of fatherhood from my past to draw upon. Thankfully, Barb had the extensive model that came from a tremendously solid and wholesome family experience. At least one of us would not be learning on the fly.

The Circle of Life and Mom's Passing

It was just a month or so before knowing about Barb's pregnancy that I learned Mom had been diagnosed with cancer. The malignancy was initially discovered in her colon but quickly moved to her liver. I did not need an official diagnosis in order to realize that Mom would not have long to live. The Middletown church was about three-and-a-half hours from where Mom lived so I was able to visit her on a number of occasions when she was ill.

The good news was that Mom had made a profession of faith in Jesus nearly two years prior. Years of observing the difference Jesus made in the lives of Alice and me had helped convince her of who He is. Grandma Salter's journey had undoubtedly also accelerated her conviction concerning Christ. By the time I visited Mom in the hospital two weeks before she passed, it was obvious she was at peace.

When we received the news of her death from Alice, we prepared to leave for the funeral. Little did we know that the few days we would spend at the memorial service and graveside burial would be filled with miracles of the most unusual sort. When all was said and done, I would again observe the mighty hand of God at work as well as His matchless grace and care.

In previous chapters, I noted our family's extremely limited means. To say Mom died poor would be an understatement. Mom died without the means to even pay for her funeral. All she had was a burial plot and gravestone that were paid for from the time Dad died. She lived off of her monthly Social Security income and each month it supplied only enough to sustain her. Alice, meanwhile, was in college and not able to contribute financially and Barb and I were living off a minimal income ourselves. No one had the thousands of dollars necessary to purchase a casket and pay for the additional funeral expenses.

It was my responsibility to figure out a way to take care of the dire financial situation, and I had no idea how to turn nothing into something. The truth is I left for her funeral knowing two things: I knew I had no ability to meet the need on my own and I knew deep inside that the Lord had an answer. Despite the gloomy situation, I had the confidence God would miraculously provide some way. Along with the complex financial need, there were other logistical things that weighed on me. Some of my Jewish family members would be present. How would we balance a memorial service that represented Mom's future hope with the fact my extended family would not participate in a Christian memorial service? Finally, there was our undependable car. Would it make the trip to New Jersey and back?

With a myriad of questions and virtually no answers, Barb, Josh (who was just over two months old), and I left for the funeral. As it would turn out, we would experience our first divine intervention before we even arrived. It was a hot day in the mid-90s on July 2. We were driving south on New Jersey Route 206 about halfway to our Millville, New Jersey, destination when our 1976 Honda Civic simply stopped functioning. I checked to see if it had overheated, but the radiator was full. Stranded on the road in the extreme heat (there were no cell phones back then and we didn't have AAA) with little money and a screaming infant, I found myself at my low point. It couldn't have been worse. I was mourning the loss of my mom. I had no means to even give her a burial and no answer to the problem of doing so. My tiny son was screaming in the heat and my car had not only resisted all attempts at starting, it made no sound at all. I did the only thing I could think of doing. I laid my hands on the broken down Honda Civic and prayed for it to be healed.

Doing such a thing would have been normal for me in my early experience when my faith was radical. But I had become somewhat sophisticated and I guess you could say even spiritually domesticated by time. Even though I possessed no real belief that anything miraculous would happen, I was desperate. To my surprise, perhaps shock would be a better word, it started right up. Many of you are reaching for a logical possible explanation concerning the car, and there may be one. All I know is the car functioned perfectly both to my destination and thereafter. My heart took it as a sign that all other matters would be resolved as well.

After arriving safely in Millville, I turned my attention to the unresolved issues that were at hand—most importantly the financial matters relating to Mom's funeral and burial. I was told that Public Assistance would take care of the financial requirements on one condition. The cemetery where Mom's previously purchased tombstone rested had to not require a burial vault. It was purchased next to Dad's at the time of his death, seventeen years earlier. My problem was I didn't know exactly where it was located other than the general vicinity of Pleasantville, New Jersey.

I was reminded of something I had never really confronted. I had never visited Dad's grave after his burial. This reminder enabled me to at least partially recognize that I had emotionally compartmentalized Dad's tragic death to the point of wanting to remove it as far as possible from my heart. At that point, it remained an unresolved wound which had left an undealt-with emotional scar.

After checking the Yellow Pages of the phone directory, I saw that there were a number of Jewish cemeteries in the area around Pleasantville and decided to call them one by one to determine whether Pearl Jaffe had a burial plot there. The very first one called responded with a yes. My faith had risen to the point that I was not shocked in the least. My next question was, "Is a burial vault required?" and the answer was no. At that point, I came to sense again that the Lord was with me and that all remaining matters would be just as easily resolved.

And they were. We had a wonderful Christian memorial service for Mom officiated by Alice's pastor. It was an uplifting testimony to the faithfulness of God. The only negative was Josh's determination to scream at the top of his eleven-week old lungs throughout the service. On the next morning, we had a separate graveside service at the Jewish cemetery. That service was only attended by Alice, Barb, Josh, my Uncle Leo

(Mom's twin brother,) his wife Rae, my faithful friend Steve Espamer, the officiating rabbi, and myself. The graveside service stood in stark contrast to the uplifting memorial service of the day before. It was somber with no hope of an afterlife. The rabbi spoke words that reflected upon life and asked questions about it that he was unable to answer. At the conclusion of the brief and impersonal service, I recited the same Mourner's *Kaddish* prayer in Hebrew that I had years earlier for Dad and Grand Pop Salter.

When all was over and the three of us set out for Middletown, I returned with a significantly increased confidence in God. As we drove home there was no fear of an automotive breakdown. The God who was with us in every element of our trip would remain with us as we returned.

I also came away with a renewed appreciation of the circle of life. My parents were gone but Josh represented life's continuation. A chapter of my life had been fully written, but new chapters were about to begin. I only could sit back and wonder what would be in store for the rest of my journey.

A Second Blessing from God

As Barb and I neared completion of our fifth year of ministry at Trinity Assembly, we learned that she was pregnant again. Both of us felt certain that our second child would be a boy as well, and we were eagerly anticipating this blessing of our next child. Our new arrival wouldn't be born in Middletown, New York, however.

Nearly five years after beginning our ministry in Middletown, I began experiencing the urge to be a senior pastor of a congregation. I conveyed this desire to my district superintendent, and it was not long before I was being considered as a candidate for a church plant near the Syracuse area. One month later, I was mutually selected by both the district officials and the new fledgling congregation. Both Barb and I felt that the Lord was leading us in this direction, and all that remained was to inform Pastor Jerry Bricker and the congregation at Trinity.

The task of informing my pastor and congregation would prove more difficult than I imagined. Our five years in Middletown were wonderful years in every respect. We had a wealth of relationships that included the youth group and congregation at large. In addition, I had an exceedingly close friendship with Pastor Jerry. I told Jerry a few days prior to telling the congregation. He graciously suggested that I preach during the Sunday morning service and then make the announcement at the conclusion of the message.

When the Sunday of my announcement arrived, I preached as planned. I cannot remember either the message's title or the biblical text. All I can remember is the announcement. I couldn't get through it without crying. I'm sure it was as painful to watch as it was to deliver. In retrospect, painful farewells are good things even though they are sad occasions. Good and fulfilling times will ultimately lead to painful separations.

In early June of 1984, we were on our way to a small, but beautiful, historic town called Cazenovia, a little over twenty miles or so from Syracuse, New York. As we spent the first two months getting settled, I worked hard to find a small storefront to serve as a place of worship for the three families who agreed to join us in forming a new congregation. After considerable searching a small Quonset hut used by a farmer's organization became available. We simply called it the "Grange Hall."

The service to officially install me as the church's pastor was scheduled for Monday September 10. Reverend Almon

Bartholemew, the New York district superintendent of the Assemblies of God, would be on hand to give the message to the tiny congregation. At the last minute, a potential monkey wrench was inserted into the mix. Our second child decided to come into the world a day before the service was to begin.

Ben was born in a way that was extremely eventful, but this time I will spare the details. The important thing is that he was born healthy. The only thing I will add at this point is that Barb had to miss my installation for obvious reasons.

Within two-and-a-half years, I had two precious sons who would teach me wonderful things about life. It all seemed like it came out of nowhere. Eight years prior I was single and now, I had a beautiful family. Fourteen years had gone by since I saw that poster on the wall that declared, "Today Is the First Day of the Rest of Your Life" and no saying could have been more meaningful, I thought. God had been so good.

So often we take the Lord's goodness for granted and fail to appreciate the many ways He brings blessing into our lives. These blessings come in large and small packages. They can be perceived as large and significant or be simple things that may even go unnoticed. But they are blessings nonetheless. We must learn how to appreciate as many as possible, recognizing that they are wonderful gifts from the gracious hand of God.

Chapter 19
From Then until Now

"Therefore I tell you, do not worry about your life, what you will eat or drink; or about your body, what you will wear. Is not life more than food, and the body more important than clothes? Look at the birds of the air; they do not sow or reap or store away in barns, and yet your heavenly Father feeds them. Are you not much more valuable than they? Can any one of you by worrying add a single hour to your life? And why do you worry about clothes? See how the lilies of the field grow. They do not labor or spin. Yet I tell you that not even Solomon in all his splendor was dressed like one of these. If that is how God clothes the grass of the field, which is here today and tomorrow is thrown into the fire, will he not much more clothe you—you of little faith? So do not worry saying, 'What shall we eat?' or 'What shall we drink?' or 'What shall we wear?' For the pagans run after all these things, and your heavenly Father knows that you need them. But seek first his kingdom and his righteousness, and all these things will be given to you as well."

—Matthew 6:25–33

"Life is a succession of lessons which must be lived to be understood."

—Unknown

I often use the metaphor of a puzzle when describing how human beings struggle with life. Humanity's fallen state leaves people with missing pieces that make it impossible for them to form a complete puzzle. As a result, they struggle to successfully navigate relationships and the necessities of life in general. Living in a world that is fallen accentuates the problem. Humans are born into this world with many of these missing pieces and more come through the hurts inflicted by others.

Matthew records Christ's observation of the human dilemma in chapter 9 of his Gospel. "When he saw the crowds, he had compassion on them, because they were harassed and helpless, like sheep without a shepherd" (v. 36). The descriptive terms *harassed* and *helpless* indicate a notion of extreme vulnerability. The multitudes were wounded to the point of being unable to find their way.

The good news for those who give their lives to Jesus is that He has all the missing pieces. There is absolutely nothing missing He cannot supply. Believers can trust in the truth that day-by-day, month by month, and year by year, He will supply all that is necessary for the healing of their lives as they seek to live obediently in His presence.

That is my testimony. The day I gave my life to Jesus, He began the lifelong process of supplying the pieces necessary to make me a whole person. Most of these were supplied apart from my conscious knowledge, but over and over it would occur to me that a fear that at one time gripped me was gone, a feeling of inferiority had dissipated, or a sense of inadequacy was no longer present. As years went by, the Spirit of God gave me confidence, an understanding of my value to Him and others, as well as the ability to love people. I am in awe of His grace, mercy, and power.

About God and People

When I think about the time that has come and gone, I think about the people God placed in my path. A great percentage of these people were individuals encountered through ministry. More than thirty-six years of full time vocational ministry provide vast opportunities to engage people in their tragedies, triumphs, and day-to-day existence. For whatever reason, I often found myself able to see these individuals through my own life's joys and struggles.

Although the people with whom my life has intersected have been varied, they overwhelmingly possessed many of the same character qualities. They have been loving individuals who deeply desired to live faithful lives. In addition, the large majority have been teachable and humble, the kind of people pastors love to have in the congregations they lead.

Jesus on one occasion was asked, "Teacher, which is the greatest commandment in the Law?" He responded, " 'Love the Lord your God with all your heart and with all your soul and with all your mind.' This is the first and greatest commandment. And the second is like it: 'Love your neighbor as yourself.' All the Law and the Prophets hang on these two commandments" (Matthew 22:36-40). Since "all the Law and the Prophets hang on these two commandments," it should be obvious that our ministries must as well.

Loving God and loving people are the essence of any faithful ministry. These God-ordained principles also make ministry joyful and fulfilling. While the pursuit of power, prestige, and position are always incredible lures, they do not set the heart free. Instead they become a huge black hole that can never be satisfied. By contrast, loving and serving God and people rather than our personal self-centered desires is liberating to the spirit.

Through the many years of ministry, I have found people

to be very much like myself. The more I understood myself, the more I understood people. Our backgrounds vary, but we share the same essential struggles. The pieces missing in the lives of others do not possess the identical shape of my own, but they do share similar edges and gaps. Our ultimate needs are fundamentally the same.

Caz Assembly

Cazenovia Assembly of God (or Caz Assembly for short) became the one and only church plant of my ministry. Cazenovia could not be referred to as a "bedroom community" in the way one typically uses the term. It is a historic village that officially dates back to the 1790s and was settled some time before. When we were there, 1984 through 2001, it had a few more than three thousand village inhabitants and roughly six thousand people total, counting the surrounding township. It lay snuggled between the more populated suburbs of Syracuse, New York, to the north and west and sprawling dairy farms to the south and east.

The village of Cazenovia is postcard quaint. The architecture of many of the homes resembles New England Cape Cod dwellings. A large lake with a sand beach borders the western side of the village. Throughout the summer, sailboats fill Caz Lake and an adjoining park with a bandstand offered a regular Thursday night seasonal concert series. A small college is located in the village center.

Cazenovia is a truly wonderful place for a young family to raise children. We were very blessed. Barb and I would regularly walk from our parsonage on the eastern side of the village through the charming downtown, each pushing a stroller, one occupied with Josh and the other with Ben. We would generally go as far as the park by the lake, stopping to hang out for a little while before making the trip back. Summers were brief in upstate New York, but extremely pleasant. This stood in stark contrast to the winters, which were long and snow covered. The Syracuse area where we lived averaged close to 130 inches of snow annually. Winters were the only drawback to an otherwise wonderful environment.

As nice as the village of Cazenovia was for us to live in, nice is also a good way to describe its people. The inhabitants of the village and surrounding town ranged from middle class to relatively wealthy in terms of its socioeconomic status. Although most of the people knew one another because their families had a significant history in the area, we never felt like outsiders. When Barb and I arrived to start the church, we never felt unwelcomed by the community.

Church plantings in a community like Cazenovia can be more challenging than most however. Part of this had to do with the village's socioeconomic quality, while another had to do with it being an historic small village. People had long histories with their respective churches which were longtime components of the community. The individuals that ultimately became a part of our fledgling congregation mostly lived outside the village in the surrounding townships.

The Quonset hut we rented from the farmer's grange was located in the southern part of the village. It cost us only forty-five dollars per week, and we were allowed to use it all day on Sunday which meant we could hold both morning and evening services there. It was rough but it serviced us well for the first few years. In time, we gradually grew, incorporated, and became a permanent congregation of deeply committed individuals and families.

Son Number Three

Six years into our time at Cazenovia, Barb became pregnant again. Even though we were surprised to learn of the soon-to-be addition, we welcomed the prospect of a third child. Throughout the pregnancy, we wondered whether we would have a daughter or another son. We were so curious in fact that we did regular surveys of people we knew or knew of whose first two children were the same gender. Our nonscientific data demonstrated that the third child turned out to be of the same gender as the first two about 75 percent of the time. Then, of course, there was that desire in my heart for three sons that I mentioned previously. With that "factual" information in our possession, we prepared for our third son.

In the spring of 1990 we discovered that a third son it would be. His birth would however be an extremely eventful experience, one that would provide more excitement than we desired. The two of us arrived in plenty of time at the hospital, and all seemed to be going well until he was born. Because he was delivered so quickly, he developed breathing complications. One attending nurse grabbed him and immediately rushed out of the delivery room, while another nurse and the doctor tried to reassure us. We were in a state of panic, not knowing whether he would live or die. A short time later the doctor and nurse returned to tell us that he was fine. He was placed in the neo-natal intensive care and remained there for a number of days before he could be released.

Barb and I could not decide whether to name him Nathan or Joel. We ultimately agreed on Nathan Joel. God had blessed us with a third son six years after our second. Our family quiver was full and we were excited at the prospect of raising three boys to the glory of God. Again, I resolved to place another figurative stone among my remembrances of divine provision. The dream of having three sons was realized. God is so good.

Building and Growing

By the time Nathan came into the world, Caz Assembly had been making slow and steady progress. We moved from the Grange Hall to the Cazenovia High School auditorium for our Sunday morning services. About five years into the church plant, we able to purchase thirty acres of property on a corner lot for only forty-five thousand dollars. We sold two lots and essentially kept twenty-two acres of the property for next to nothing. This acreage consisted of approximately 1,400 feet of combined road frontage.

A couple of years later we built the church building and moved into the facility. Our growing congregation was filled with excitement as we worshipped in our new home for the first time. We met on a concrete slab and used metal folding chairs for seating. As a result the acoustics were atrocious. All that did not matter to anyone there because our congregation for the first time had a sense of permanence.

A church is not about property and buildings of course. It is about people, and the Lord brought us some of the most wonderful individuals and families. They came from all walks of life and religious backgrounds, and were committed to me as their pastor, one another, and most importantly Jesus. Some had been committed believers for some time, others were relatively new believers who came to faith as a result of the church's ministry.

Because many of the families of the church were our age, our sons had numerous friends from within the congregation. I would often reflect on how different their childhood and adolescence was to my own. I was so very thankful for that reality. While I had virtually no male role models in my life when I needed it most, our boys had so many. Our church family had a significant number of men and all of them were so willing to be influences to the young boys of our congregation.

Not only did the church have numerous men who were dedicated to its young boys, the boys thoroughly enjoyed their company. This was especially evident to Barb and me when Josh and Ben became teenagers. The families of our congregation had a great deal of fun when they were together. Picnics, softball games, boat rides on the lake, holiday celebrations, and other events filled our lives. Our children enjoyed growing up in the environment that accompanied our Cazenovia experience.

Barb and I enjoyed our church community as well. Many members became some of our closest friends. There is just something about being in the same stage of life that can enable people to become close. As leaders of the congregation, Barb and I found ourselves in the position of sharing the joys and sorrows of the precious people God brought into our lives. We discovered how good it felt to be close to the people we were attempting to lead spiritually.

Personally, the friends I made spanned a significant spectrum of personalities and interests. Some were real sports fans like me, while others were avid campers and outdoorsmen, unlike me. What they all had in common was that they were men of solid and growing spiritual character. When we spent time together, there was nearly always some spiritual take away.

As it would happen, one of my friends loved baseball in the same way I did. I met Glenn when his wife Lisa invited Barb and me over for dinner. Lisa had just begun to attend the church and Glenn at the time was not overly interested. Her hope was that perhaps her husband and I would somehow hit it off. It turned out that Glenn was a passionate Yankees fan to the degree that I loved the Phillies. We spent the evening impressing one another with our respective knowledge base of baseball in general and our teams in particular. Each of us could discuss our teams dating back decades. Glenn started coming to church immediately after that evening and we became great friends. The two of us went on a number of road trips which included traveling to Yankees Stadium, Veterans Stadium in Philly, and Fenway Park in Boston.

These years were also wonderful bonding times with my boys. I had the privilege of coaching Josh, Ben, and Nate in varying levels of baseball. When Josh and Ben entered high school, I also coached their junior varsity basketball teams. I can't describe how much I enjoyed this part of my life. Whether or not they enjoyed it, well, maybe you would have to ask them.

When it comes to shared interests, the boys are both similar and different. Josh and Ben are both sports fans like me, while Nate is not. Like me, Josh and Nate love to follow politics, which is something Ben tends to avoid. It is amusing to me that each share my interests in unique and varying ways. Josh is a New York sports fan having grown up in New York, while Ben joins me in having Philadelphia loyalties.

Ironically, this led to an odd occasion of déjà vu that reminded me of a significant past memory. It involved my lifelong love of the Philadelphia Phillies. In an earlier chapter, I recalled the occasion when my Phillies lost the 1964 pennant on the last day of the season and my father had to comfort me in my deep sorrow. An unnervingly similar thing happened when Ben was nine. The Phils, beat the Braves in the 1993 playoffs in exciting fashion and advanced to the World Series against the Toronto Blue Jays. The series went back and forth, and entering the sixth game the Phillies were down three games to two. Needing to win to extend the series to a seventh and final game, they were ahead 9-7 in the Blue Jays' bottom of the ninth. In horror, we watched Joe Carter of the Jays hit a three-run homer off Phils' reliever Mitch Williams and tragically end the Phillies season once again. This time, it was me comforting my son as my father had comforted me.

Suffering, Sorrow, and Joy

Life is never free from times of adversity, many of which can be deeply painful. Our family experienced one of those extremely difficult periods in 1997 and 1998. Barb's family was in the midst of planning a celebration commemorating her parents' fiftieth wedding anniversary. It was to be a large dinner gathering celebrating their fifty years of marriage and was to include the extended family and a large number of their friends. Everyone was eagerly anticipating the event.

A couple of weeks prior to the event, Olga, Barb's mom, called with disturbing news. She had been experiencing difficulties with her legs and her hands to the point that a number of basic functions were becoming impaired. She had seen a doctor who made an appointment with a specialist. The doctor had discussed some of the possibilities with her and most of them were not good. The potential diagnoses of a brain tumor, Lou Gehrig's disease, or other disorders involving muscles and nerves were all scary to the entire family. When Barb asked me what Lou Gehrig's disease was, I remember my response. "Anything but that" were my words.

The anniversary celebration went on while the family awaited the specialist's appointment. It was a wonderful evening featuring numerous tributes, family pictures, and the abundance of deeply moving expressions of love. As everyone outwardly was experiencing feelings of joy, the immediate family was deeply troubled over the possible news that loomed. There was a nagging sense of dread.

The news came just a few days after the celebration. It ended up being the worst possible outcome. Barb's mom was diagnosed with Amyotrophic Lateral Sclerosis better known as ALS or Lou Gehrig's disease, named after the famous New York Yankees first baseman. ALS is a progressive disorder of the nervous system and always fatal. It paralyzes the muscles, eventually disabling all muscle movement including the ability to breathe.

Olga lived approximately a year after the initial diagnosis. The year became a deeply spiritual experience for the family. This was especially true for Barb, her dad, her siblings, and of course her mom. During the year of 1998, we made a number of trips to see her mom and dad. Barb's mom and dad always attempted to be positive and dealt with the adversity of their circumstances with incredible courage. Despite the difficulty of watching Barb's mom deteriorate physically, we repeatedly left for home with a conviction that God was present and working in every person's life.

As the illness progressed, Barb's mom gradually lost the ability to function. It was not long before she became unable to speak. But as bad as things got, there was always laughter and cheer in the home whenever we came to visit. A few months before the end, Barb made weeklong trips by train to help her dad care for her mom. Nate, who was eight years old at the time and was being homeschooled, went with her. The rest of us stayed in New York because I could not leave the church for the more lengthy stays and the boys were in school.

Barb's sisters, Patty and Karen, and brother Bob often spoke of their desire to give back to their mom the love and care they had received from her their entire lives. Olga was an extremely giving person, especially when it came to her children and grandchildren. Her illness provided a tremendous opportunity for them to return the devotion they had received. Patty, Karen, Barb, and Bob took turns helping their dad to give extended care to their mom during the final months.

When it looked like the end was near, Barb and Nate made what they thought would be one final trip to Indiana to be at her side. Our entire family had just made the trip to see her a couple of weeks prior. As it turned out, the end was not quite at hand and Barb and Nate had to return home. Just after they had returned, a final phone call came stating that she was hours away from passing. Barb and Nate went immediately back to Indiana by train and got there just in time to share in the final hours of her life.

What took place during those hours left an incredible impact on all who were present. According to the family, the presence of God was manifested in ways that no one could appreciate who wasn't there. Peace filled the room as worship songs played. Those at the bedside experienced the Lord in ways that continue to shape their lives. While Josh, Ben, and I weren't able to be there for Olga's passing (we arrived two days later for the funeral), I am very thankful that Barb and Nate could experience the unique blessing of God that will always live in their memories. God has a way of bringing peace and joy in the midst of the greatest sorrow.

From Pastor to Professor

The seventeen years we spent in Cazenovia in many ways seemed to us to go by in a flash. In the spring of 2000, Josh graduated high school and was ready for college. Josh had three Christian universities at the top of his list and, after visiting two of them with me, he settled on Evangel University in Springfield, Missouri. Since Springfield is where Barb and I went to college, I am sure that Josh sensed that it was our first choice for him, but the decision was his.

When Barb and I drove Josh to Springfield and then returned home without him, it was one of those monumental life occasions. Letting go of our firstborn was really an emotional event. We entrusted him to the Lord and left for home with a hole in our hearts. It is one thing to understand that some things are a part of life and quite another to fully accept it, but we tried and ultimately succeeded.

About the same time, I began to feel that God was planting a seed in my heart to experience a life change myself. I enrolled in a doctoral program at the Assemblies of God Theological Seminary, feeling God was leading me to teach Bible and practical theology on the college level. The classwork segment of the program was modular and only required that I attend classes on-site four weeks annually. The seminary was also in Springfield, which gave me the opportunity to spend time with Josh while I was there.

I also applied and sent résumés to a number of colleges within the Assemblies of God, requesting consideration for faculty positions within my area of expertise. Unfortunately, all replied by thanking me for applying but they had no openings in my field. I accepted the responses as from the Lord, but still deeply felt that a change was imminent.

Then it happened. I was at the end of my morning class at the seminary during the winter module when I discovered that the vice president for academic affairs at Central Bible College, my alma mater, was waiting for me outside of class. Central Bible College, Evangel University, and the Assemblies of God Theological Seminary at the time represented the national Bible college, liberal arts university, and theological seminary of the denomination and were located in its headquarters city. He asked if I could have lunch with him and later asked if I would be willing to interview for a faculty position. From that moment, I knew that our lives would be taking a new direction. I called Barb that evening and she knew as well. Even though a series of interviews would follow, we were certain of the result.

Leaving Cazenovia was very difficult. We loved the congregation, the village, and everything about central New York (except the winters, of course). Seventeen years allows you to forge a significant number of wonderful relationships, and we would miss our people dearly. We were certain that this was God's direction, however. Just as we had in Middletown many years before, we cried before the congregation and prepared ourselves for the new aspect of our journey. And, it would be great to be in the same city as Josh once more.

On August 5, 2001, our family arrived in Springfield. Barb and I had chosen a home during one of our previous scheduled interviews, and Ben and Nathan were seeing it for the first time. When they saw it, they weren't at all impressed to say the least, mostly because they loved the parsonage in Cazenovia. It was the only home they had known, and they were suffering the same sense of loss as we were.

Barb took a position as administrative coordinator for Chaplaincy, the Assemblies of God's endorsing body for all its military, institutional, and occupational chaplains, and I began my first semester of teaching. It all went seamlessly. Barb enjoyed her work and I loved teaching young people who felt a vocational call to ministry. We were in the center of God's will and there is no greater place.

The Privilege of Influence

More than fourteen years have come and gone since that fall of 2001, and much has taken place during that time. The tragedy of 9/11 happened two weeks into my first semester.

Josh met a wonderful girl named Brooke and was married in 2004. Ben met an equally wonderful girl named Rachael and was married in 2005. We have five beautiful and pugnacious grandchildren named Harrison, Adelynn, Samuel, Titus, and Lily. Nathan is not married yet. He recently completed his last year in engineering school and, at the time of this writing, has accepted an engineering position in of all places Fairbanks, Alaska, where he now lives.

I spent twelve years at Central Bible College, the last six as the Church Ministries department chair. In 2013 Central Bible College, Evangel University, and the Assemblies of God Theological Seminary were consolidated into one university retaining the title Evangel University. The seminary retained its identity as an embedded seminary within the university and kept its name intact. As a result of the consolidation, I currently hold the title of department chair and professor in Church Leadership and Preaching at Evangel University.

The fourteen years or so at Central Bible College and Evangel University have been wonderful in so many respects. Along with the obvious blessings that accompany the growth in our family, has been the ability to fulfill a God-given passion, the passion to teach young people who have answered a call to vocational ministry. During this time, I have experienced the privilege of having a part in the spiritual and intellectual development of thousands of students who have gone to hundreds of communities in the United States and every inhabited continent of the world. I have taught, mentored, and counseled precious individuals who will expand the kingdom of God in ways that exceed my ability to imagine.

Over the years, my mind has often reflected on the days of my youth, when there was no apparent hope for my life to have any real significance whatsoever. I was a child and adolescent whose home was utterly broken. I was the son of a father who had lost hope to the point of taking his life, of a mother who had emotionally withdrawn to the point of barely coping. In 2004, when I completed my doctorate, I reminded myself that prior to my salvation, I graduated from high school near the back of my class and failed my first semester at my local community college earning three Fs and a D. I often ask, "How did it come to this? How did I get from there to here?" I can only come to one answer—the wonderful and manifest grace of God. He is fully able to not only save a person's soul, but also to transform that same person's destiny. When God saves individuals, He receives glory from the life transformations that result, both in the lives of those He saves and in those who are influenced by them to grow in their own participation in His eternal kingdom.

Chapter 20

A Grateful Heart

"Praise the LORD, my soul;
all my inmost being, praise his holy name.
Praise the LORD, my soul,
and forget not all his benefits—
who forgives all your sins
and heals all your diseases,
who redeems your life from the pit
and crowns you with love and compassion,
who satisfies your desires with good things
so that your youth is renewed like the eagle's."
—Psalm 103:1–5

"What shall I return to the LORD
for all his goodness to me?
I will lift up the cup of salvation
and call on the name of the LORD.
—Psalm 116:12–13

Attitude may not be everything in life, but it is pretty close. A positive attitude creates an optimistic perspective that tends to set healthy boundaries for our patterns of thinking, while a negative outlook does the reverse. Life goes so much better when we focus on the amount of liquid that is in the glass instead of the amount that is missing.

I believe the greatest variable in a person's attitude is the practice of gratitude. I call it a practice because it must be practiced. Gratitude is a discipline no different than prayer, healthy eating, or a solid work ethic. It is a regular choice we make to observe all that is good about life and remembering to thank the God who provided these blessings.

It has been more than forty-five years since that monumental afternoon in Bob's bedroom when I made a profession of faith in Jesus as Lord and Savior. During these years, God had blessed me with so much. I am so glad that I do not have to imagine what life would have become had Christ not intervened in my lifeless and helpless state. There are countless blessings of my Christ-life that are the direct result of God's restorative power.

Freedom

My mind occasionally recalls that first night of the Woodstock Rock Festival when Richie Havens sang his famous improvised rendition of "Freedom." Hundreds of thousands of people, including me, proclaimed our emancipation from government, rules, and anything perceived by us to be bondage. In the ethos of the moment, we declared ourselves free from all who would oppress us. What we did not realize at the time, and many still do not, was that the essential source of bondage does not come from without but rather from within.

At the United States Medical Center for Federal Prisoners, I regularly minister to men who are inwardly free although outwardly incarcerated. Conversely, the world outside is filled with those who are free from such external chains but are inwardly bound. True incarceration and liberation are spiritual matters. Jesus proclaimed this truth clearly in John's Gospel when He declared to those who were challenging His message, "If you hold to my teaching, you are really my disciples. Then you will know the truth, and the truth will set you free. . . . Very truly I tell you, everyone who sins is a slave of sin. Now a slave has no permanent place in the family, but a son belongs to it forever. So if the Son sets you free, you will be free indeed" (John 8:31–32, 34–36).

What the false promises of Woodstock could not hope to do for me, Jesus did. Jesus brought freedom to me in many different ways. I gradually became liberated from external habits, negative thoughts, and deep emotional and psychological wounds. As the years passed, this freedom enabled me to increasingly appropriate God's truth, which progressively renewed my mind and liberated my heart. I am so grateful to God for His liberating power, through His Holy Spirit.

Meaning

Prior to that afternoon in October 1970, my life could not have been more meaningless. It could have been amply described by Bob Dylan in his classic song, "Like a Rolling Stone" when he asked,

"How does it feel . . .
To be on your own…
with no direction…
Like a rolling stone?"

To be without Jesus is to be without a compass, a North Star, and focal point. In my situation, there were little or no resources to affirm, guide and direct. For me, meaning was only about finding something that would make the moment matter.

When it came to how I viewed myself, it was clear that I

didn't matter much. There was the deep sense that if I ceased to exist, few would be impacted. Without question my mom, sister, and grandma would grieve, but who else? I felt the world would be no worse off without me. Thomas Carlyle once said, "The man without a purpose is like a ship without a rudder—a waif, a nothing, a no man."

The grace of God changed all that, and I recognized the difference almost immediately. Once a person realizes he matters to God, that person realizes he matters. The truth is affirmed again and again by the indwelling Holy Spirit. The truth was also reaffirmed by the precious people of Chestnut Assembly whom I referred to in previous chapters. The evidence began accumulating in my life. I mattered to God, the people of Chestnut Assembly, my friends, my wife who loved me dearly, my sons, the people to whom I ministered on a day-to-day basis, my grandchildren, my students; I could go on and on. Again, thank you Lord for the gift of meaning.

Wholeness

It is a wonderful thing that the God who saves us does not leave us broken. He doesn't simply save our souls and leave our wounded lives unaffected. Sin has a devastating impact on people. It robs people of their hope for a future. It not only destroys peoples' relationships, but it diminishes their ability to even form them. Sin leaves people wounded in their hearts and often in their bodies as well.

By contrast, Jesus progressively brings about the restoration of the entirety of our human selves. He sends His Spirit to bind up the brokenhearted, turn the ashes of life into beauty, replace mourning with the oil of joy, and transform despair into praise (Isaiah 61:2–3). Jesus put it this way, "The thief [Satan] comes only to steal and kill and destroy; I have come that they may have life, and have it to the full" (John 10:10).

Wholeness in practical terms includes a person's sense of value, worth, and confidence. It enables that person to have what I like to call a soft and flexible quality that enables him or her to withstand the relational challenges that life inevitably brings. The whole person is at peace and therefore able to share that peace with others. Perpetual conflict and drama progressively give way to a growing calm and serenity.

While we are all in process when it comes to the healing of our hearts, I am so thankful for the incredible power of God to repair wounds. Many years after my father's tragic suicide, I remained unable to emotionally connect with that painful period of my life. Gradually, however I became able to speak of it publicly and share its relationship to the person I am today. Over the years, I found myself able to minister to people who endured similar experiences and help them through the lingering hurt and irrational feelings of shame. I went from a person hiding a secret to one who could minister wholeness.

My Life Partner and Best Friend

My teenage years were by far the loneliest period of my life. My friendships, with precious few exceptions, were shallow and superficial. The overall lack of family support left me lacking any sense of value. As I stated previously, subconsciously I came to believe that good things were for other people and not for me. As I progressed to my late teenage years, the "good things" came to mean a girlfriend.

Then came Jesus and with Jesus automatically came hope. At first this hope had to do with life in general, but before too long, it would also increasingly come to mean a special girl with whom I could spend my life. God knew my heart and provided me with a gift that is beyond all earthly gifts. Barb is my life partner and best friend.

Love is meant to increase through the years and in my case it most certainly has. Love doesn't just happen; it is the result of the effort we put in. A healthy marriage is dependent upon the participants' ability to extend and receive love. It is essential to realize that this ability is not automatic. It is the natural result of each individual's own spiritual growth and development.

My wife has always had the amazing ability to absorb those things that were lacking in me. While she would likely say that there was little to absorb, I think that there was more than she realized. Barb has a peaceful and serene personality that enables her to make adjustments and understand the relevant issues in our relationship.

Barb often tells me that I have been an easy person to love, and I'm glad she feels that way. I certainly feel the same way about her. Perhaps those mutual feelings of contentment are vital in a happy marriage. If so, I'm thankful that we have made our life partnership the deep friendship it is.

Friendship presupposes a joy of simply being together. At times it includes serious conversation, but at other times not. For the most part, it is just about presence. Generally speaking, there is something that just feels empty about doing things without her. Having her with me makes everything else in life more enjoyable. The love of a special woman and the love I can share in return together represent a blessing that requires deep gratitude to the Lord.

Fatherhood

I've discussed the impact my father's passing had on various aspects of my life. It has been clear to me over the years that this was the signature event of my early life. There were two aspects to the significance of Dad's death. The first was that he simply wasn't there when I needed his influence so desperately. The second had to do with the manner of his passing. He did not have to die—he chose to die.

All through my teenage years, I wanted a father. A boy needs a male mentor in his life and when things looked especially bleak, I found myself most acutely aware of this need. Unfortunately, there were no surrogate fathers who made themselves available, so I was simply rudderless.

My salvation changed all that. Gradually, I came to understand that I was no longer fatherless. My Heavenly Father had adopted me and provided me with all that I had missed and much more. The Psalmist's words came true: "A father to the fatherless, a defender of widows, is God in his holy dwelling" (Psalm 68:5).

When it became clear that God was going to provide me with the blessing of child, I was all in. The prospect of fatherhood was a huge deal to me, and extraordinarily meaningful from the first moments. It was an opportunity to be to my sons all that I had missed. What I lacked in terms of knowledge, I tried to make up for in desire.

All three of my sons are exceedingly precious to me. They are the most wonderful gifts and represent so much of my life's meaning. Now that they are grown, I miss them when we are separated. One lives a little over two hundred miles away and another halfway around the world. My third son recently moved to Fairbanks, Alaska. When we are together, it is always a joyful occasion.

Each of my boys represents a special manifestation of divine grace. As I watch Josh and Ben engage their respective roles as fathers, I am amazed at how attentive they are to their children. It gives me tremendous pleasure to watch their devotion to parenthood. Nate amazes me in an altogether different way. Although possessing a real interest in math and science, he went to a small Christian high school that was not equipped to give him the background necessary for engineering, his desired field of study. Despite this, he persisted to the point of earning a place on the Dean's List. Nate has learned the character quality of perseverance. I am proud of each of my sons' accomplishments and will refrain from highlighting them further even though I could list many.

Most importantly, all my sons are devoted to Christ and active in His kingdom. While they are successful in many respects, their dedication to living for Jesus is that which gives me by far the greatest joy. I am thankful they saw enough of Christ in our home to enable them to pursue His kingdom in the way they have.

Legacy

It didn't hit me early on, but after some years I began to realize that my life transformation by the grace of God could be the beginning of a family legacy. Actually, this didn't occur to me until my oldest two sons were married and began to have children of their own. Because my heritage is Jewish, it is quite possible that I am the first person in the family's history to know Christ. Outside of the first century, Jews coming to Jesus is a relatively new phenomenon. In other words, my story will be the first in a lineage of generations who will follow and serve Jesus.

As my mind wanders, I wonder, how will my descendants serve God's glorious kingdom? Will they serve as pastors, missionaries, Christian physicians, educators, or tradesmen? What roles will they play in the furtherance of the Lord's eternal purposes? As I look at my grandchildren, I dream of their participation in the most awesome enterprise that has ever existed. My heart reflects upon how it all began on that October afternoon in 1970. I further contemplate that although my life once was aimless, purposeless, and useless, now it is not only significant for me but for future generations.

The legacy has already begun to take shape. I watch my sons and daughters-in-law teach my grandsons and granddaughters about Jesus and how serving Him is the most important thing in the world. And as I watch them, my heart fills once again with gratitude.

Eternal Life

Although everything I have mentioned is exceedingly wonderful, they all pale in comparison to the truth that I will spend eternity in the presence of the One "who loved me and gave himself for me" (Galatians 2:20). Followers of Jesus are not only blessed in this life in uncounted ways, but they will experience an unspeakable joyful eternity (1 Peter 1:8). We currently only see "a reflection as in a mirror," but one day we will be able to fully absorb the glory of it all (1 Corinthians 13:12).

A mirror in biblical times was not like the kind of mirrors with which we are familiar. They were more like polished metal that gave poor representations of the actual. The theological terminology that we use to describe the nature of our relationship to Christ is extremely useful, but it cannot compare to what will be. For instance, I know from God's Word that I am an adopted son of God, but I do not come close to fully apprehending the incredible reality I will one day experience. I do know that I will understand "fully, even as I am fully known" (1 Corinthians 13:12), but I have no idea what that experience will be like.

Life has taught me that God always exceeds my expectations. Heaven will do so in ways beyond my comprehension.

My guess is that it will reveal shades of color not yet seen and variations of pitch my ears have never heard. Heaven will reveal the impact of my life on others, and even the impact of my children, grandchildren, and all the generations to come. All of these things will make the joy unspeakable.

Most of all, of course, heaven will be heaven because of the presence of Jesus. One look into His eyes will reveal that His love for me was infinitely greater than I ever realized. It will place all pain and suffering in context. My many questions will be answered to my complete satisfaction and worship will fill my heart far beyond anything expressible.

Lost and Found

While there is so much yet to be learned, I have learned much. I know what it means to be lost and what it means to be found. The difference is like night and day, black and white, and crying and laughing. It is like the difference between being gravely ill and being in the best of health.

The state of being lost is filled with loneliness and emptiness. You feel estranged and alienated from your Creator and to varying degrees the people in your life. In the best case scenario, you feel guilty; in the worst, you lose any sense of guilt for your actions. You wander about attempting to fill your life with temporary pleasures, most of which will eventually have a payday—a bad payday.

When a person is lost, that person is in rebellion with his or her Creator. The individual knows something is wrong, but pushes it to the back of the mind. The lost person is unresponsive to God, but all the while convinced of his or her goodness. Wrong is justified, excused, or hidden. People are hurt, but no matter; it is rationalized as simply part of the hardness of life.

The state of being found is altogether different. You feel

God's presence within. You grow in your understanding of your Creator and recognize that happiness comes from giving, serving, and loving. Guilt gives way to hope, rebellion to submission to God, self-centeredness to sacrifice, and emptiness to worship. There is no bad payday ahead, only assurance of eternal life.

When a person is found, it is not because that person finds God. Rather it is because God has found that person. As a result, sin is not pushed back into the recesses of the mind, it is confessed to a loving Father and repented of. The found person has no false sense of goodness, only a deep appreciation for the grace of God.

Being found is like finding the hope that eluded you, the closeness you always dreamed of and the father you always wanted. It doesn't answer all your questions but convinces you that they will find an ultimate answer. Being found is experiencing the Master Puzzle Maker supplying all your missing puzzle pieces. There is nothing like being found.

As I reflect upon my life's journey, my heart is filled with praise. That praise can be summed up in the words of the Psalmist:

> Praise the LORD, my soul;
> all my inmost being, praise his holy name.
> Praise the LORD, my soul,
> and forget not all his benefits---
> who forgives all your sins
> and heals all your diseases,
> who redeems your life from the pit
> and crowns you with love and compassion,
> who satisfies your desires with good things
> so that your youth is renewed like the eagle's . . .
> Praise the LORD, my soul.
> Psalm 103:1–5, 22

Afterword

Cousin Albert

It was late in 2012 when I received an entirely unexpected phone call. It was from a cousin that I had neither seen nor heard from for close to fifty years. Albert Geiger was the son and only child of my Aunt Mildred, my father's younger sister (see chapter 1). He was and still is living in North Carolina.

Albert is ten years my senior. As best as I can remember, I was about ten or eleven when I last remember seeing him. He was either in college or in military service and had returned home to see his mom and stepdad (Uncle Ned) when I was at my Aunt Mildred's house visiting with Dad.

In our initial phone conversation, Albert revealed that he had lost his wife a couple of years earlier and decided to contact his four cousins all of whom he hadn't seen for many years. He had been able to locate his other two cousins earlier and finally was able to find Alice and me after some additional effort. Our conversation was pleasant and we agreed to call one another on a regular basis. All this felt a little strange to me because I had lost contact with virtually all family members after Dad's death.

Albert called again about a month later, and we began exchanging calls during the months that followed. It didn't take long for us to find some mutual interests. Albert also enjoys following sports and discussing politics. More importantly however was the opportunity to reminisce about the people common to our lives, namely my dad and his mom. Our phone conversations provided a number of opportunities to do just that.

Our Reunion

Albert also established contact with Alice through phone conversations, although he and I spoke more often. The more our phone conversations developed, the more comfortable we felt as we opened up to one another. For my part, it felt good to reestablish contact with family. It was clear that I was ready to engage my past more fully.

In the spring of 2013, Albert and I decided to meet for the first time since our last encounter sometime in the early to mid-1960s. We agreed to get together in July of that year in Millville, New Jersey, where Alice lived in order for us to all meet. Vineland where all of us grew up was only six miles from Millville and that would enable us to visit the places of our early lives. I flew from Springfield into Philadelphia, and rented a car while Albert drove from his home in Winston Salem, North Carolina. Albert and I agreed to book rooms in the same motel and meet there before joining Alice.

During the plane flight, I wondered if I would even recognize my cousin, since it had been more than five decades since I laid eyes on him. Oddly enough when I saw him, I recognized him immediately. I remembered his facial features although he was of course much older. He in many ways looked similar to how I expected him to look. Although we only spent a couple of days together, the three of us felt like we took up where life had left us off. We, along with Alice's son Nicholas spent an enjoyable day in beautiful Cape May, New Jersey, and thoroughly enjoyed discussing our respective journeys through life.

Things about Dad I Never Knew

The most personally meaningful element of my reunion with my cousin was his knowledge of my father. I was extremely surprised at the extent of Albert's knowledge of my dad. In fact, the more I pondered his knowledge of my father, the more I sensed that he knew him better than I did. While I resented the thought at first, it was clear to me the reason. Albert was about ten years older than me, and he had known Dad for much longer and in an altogether different context.

Albert not only shared with me his love for my father, but he explained the reasons, reasons I had never before heard. On the evening of our second day together, we talked for quite a while in his car before retiring for the night. Albert shared the story of his childhood, explaining how my father became a father to him after his own dad was no longer in the picture. Dad took care of his sister Mildred and Albert, at times providing significant financial support, even though he had little himself. He ended by saying that Dad was a wonderful man and he would never forget him.

The words, "a wonderful man" and "never forget him" stuck in my mind. For whatever reason, I felt feelings of completion as I contemplated those words. Albert told me many other things as well about Dad and as I asked him additional questions, I became acutely aware of the fact that I no longer felt any desire to compartmentalize my memory of my father. Instead, I wanted to know all I could about him.

All this makes me more in awe of my Heavenly Father. I am so thankful that He cares about all of the things that enable us to find our complete healing. Meeting Cousin Albert was another in a list of gifts that has become magnificently long and keeps getting longer.

Afterword 2

A Baseball Reprise

In various parts of my story, I have alluded to the role baseball played in my relationship with my father and my relationship with my son Ben. I noted how my father comforted me in the aftermath of the disastrous ending of the Phillies 1964 season and how I comforted Ben after the Phillies lost in the sixth game of the 1993 World Series. While the Phils finally won their first World Championship during my lifetime in 1980, that was four years prior to Ben's birth, so we didn't have an opportunity to share in that joy together.

That all changed in 2008. Since 2007, Ben, Rachael, and their two young children have lived half way around the world due to his work. Our family communicates with them through Skype, Facetime, e-mail, and phone conversations. They return home approximately every two years or so. When Ben and I talk, we talk about all kinds of stuff, including our much beloved Phillies.

The 2007 baseball season began a transition for our favorite team. They won the National League East Division for the first time since losing the 1993 World Series and, as a result, went to the playoffs. Unfortunately, they lost in the first round to the Colorado Rockies, three games to none, and disappointed us once again. Ben and I consoled ourselves as usual with the words, "Maybe next year."

During the 2008 season, the Phillies were in contention throughout. They ended up repeating as the National League East champs, winning the division by three games. The big question was whether or not they could succeed in the playoffs. Ben and I were braced for another disappointment.

In the first round of the playoffs, the Phils faced the Milwaukee Brewers who were the wild Card team. The Phillies disposed of the Brewers, winning the series three games to one. Our hopes rose after the series since they had not won a playoff series since their failure in 1993. Next they had to face a very good Dodgers team. The Los Angeles Dodgers were champions of the Western Division of the National League and were a formidable match. But again the Phillies rose to the occasion and beat them in five games (four games to one).

The stage was set for a best-of-seven-game World Series with the American League champions, the Tampa Bay Rays. The Rays entered the series as the favorite due to their superior record of 97 wins and 65 losses. The Phils, on the other hand, had a more than respectable record of 92 wins and 70 losses. The teams split the first two games in Tampa, and moved to Philadelphia for the next three games. If necessary, the schedule was for the last two games of the series to be played back in the Rays' home ballpark.

Game three was close throughout and was tied going into the last of the ninth. When the Phillies won the game on a cheap infield single by catcher Carlos Ruiz, everyone was optimistic that this would finally be their year, everyone except Ben and me of course. We knew better than to be optimistic. But after the Phils trounced the Rays 10–2 in game four, it was hard to contain our enthusiasm. They only needed one more win out of the next three games.

In game five, the Phils took an early 2–0 lead in the first inning, but the Rays scored a run in the fourth and another in the sixth to tie the game at 2–2. Then an odd thing happened. Heavy storms came to the east and the rain was so heavy, the game had to be postponed. When it rained hard the next day as well, the series was delayed further. We had to wait a couple of days in order to see if we would witness our first world championship as father and son. Game five eventually resumed two days later, and Ben and I decided to check in with one another as the game progressed.

The Phillies took a 3–2 lead in the bottom of the sixth but the Rays tied it again in the top of the seventh. When the Phillies scored a run in the bottom of the seventh, they only needed to hold the Rays for two more innings. Neither team scored in the eighth inning, and going into the top of the ninth, the Phils needed only to record three more outs. The Phillies' relief pitcher was Brad Lidge who had saved every game in which he had been called upon during the entire season.

Ben called me during the ninth and we determined to stay on the line to see if we could celebrate a special memory. The Rays were able to get a man to second base with two outs and we nervously waited for the outcome. With two strikes on the hitter, Ben told me not to react at all because his telecast was on a four or five second delay. Even Barb, who is the farthest thing from a baseball fan on the face of the earth, was watching. She knew how much it meant to the two of us. When Brad Lidge struck out Eric Hinske for the win, Barb screamed and Ben knew the result a couple of seconds before he saw it. In a moment of time, the 1964 and 1993 seasons of disappointment were washed away.

Appendix

Beginning the Journey: How to Become Found and Free

You may be asking yourself, "How can I become found and experience the freedom of becoming God's child?" or "Why would God care about my life's struggle?" I want to assure you that it is natural to feel as though you are too insignificant to appear on God's radar. It is also natural to allow guilt about the past to feed the sense that you are unworthy of His intervention in your life.

Thankfully, however, it is not a matter of your worthiness of God's love and care. The truth is it is not a matter of our worthiness. It is about His nature to love those He has created. God created you and me with a purpose and that is to know Him and bring Him glory. It is never too late to fulfill that purpose. When you do, you will be found and thereby begin your journey to true freedom. Jesus put it this way, "You will know the truth, and the truth will set you free."

A further question may linger: "Where do I begin?" My purpose here is to outline a few simple but critical principles that will help you begin the journey to spiritual wholeness. Please understand—these are more principles than steps. You need to understand what God desires.

Honesty

The journey has to begin with an honest heart. You need to understand that the last thing God wants is your attempts to impress Him with your goodness or merit. Neither does He desire your justifications and excuses. He is looking for humility. The Lord wants you to offer yourself to Him just as you are.

Honesty is the foundation of any true relationship. No marriage can withstand the lack of integrity between a husband and wife. No significant relationship between parents and children can exist if any one cannot communicate honestly. The same can be said for other kinds of friendship.

We must remember that God is all knowing, He is intimately acquainted with our thoughts and motives, as well as our actions. He cannot be fooled by our insincere attempts to bargain for His favor. He is aware of every calculation on our part and will resist our pretense and deception.

But it also important to understand that the reverse is also true. When we come to Him honestly, that alone is so much more important than our accumulated failures. God will always forgive the person who comes to Him in integrity and respond to the one who sincerely calls upon His name.

Humility

Honesty ultimately must take the form of acknowledging your need before God. You need to see yourself as you truly are rather than through the rose-colored glasses you may have previously chosen. We all have blind spots and need to allow God to reveal them to us. It is so easy to see the faults in others while remaining blind to our own very serious flaws. It is vital that we understand that it is not our failures that separate us from God, but rather our refusal to acknowledge them.

This truth was clearly articulated by Jesus in His parable of the Pharisee and the tax collector found in Luke chapter 18.

> To some who were confident of their own righteousness and looked down on everyone else, Jesus told this

> parable: "Two men went up to the temple to pray, one a Pharisee and the other a tax collector. The Pharisee stood by himself and prayed: 'God, I thank you that I am not like other people—robbers, evildoers, adulterers—or even like this tax collector. I fast twice a week and give a tenth of all I get.'
>
> "But the tax collector stood at a distance. He would not even look up to heaven, but beat his breast and said, 'God have mercy on me, a sinner.'
>
> "I tell you that this man, rather than the other, went home justified before God. For all those who exalt themselves will be humbled, and those who humble themselves will be exalted." Luke 18: 9–14

In the parable, Jesus clearly reveals a critical truth. God is willing to forgive our sins providing we come to Him and humbly acknowledge them. Humility is a prerequisite for a relationship with God. It opens a window to Him that will otherwise remain shut.

The root of all sin is human pride. It blinds us to the things that not only keep us from divine forgiveness, but also healthy relationships with those we care the most about. Pride fractures marriages, harms our ability to meaningfully engage our children, destroys friendships, and most importantly separates and alienates us from our Creator.

Trust

Once we gain the true perspective about who we really are, we must then look to what God has done to free us from our dilemma. The Bible declares that we are unable to change our situation. Our natures are selfish and we lack the power to alter who we really are. There are no self-help programs that can provide the remedy. The only One who can change us is God Himself.

The Bible is clear in the way it describes the human condition. It states that we have violated God's laws and are utterly separated and alienated from Him as a result. It further states that we face judgment. But there is good news. God provided the answer by sending His one and only Son, Jesus, to pay our penalty for us. All we need to do is accept this reality and place our trust in what God has already accomplished. Jesus died on the cross for your sins and mine. In doing so, He identified with our struggle to sin and provided a way of escape.

Perhaps one of the most well-known passages in the Bible is John 3:16: "For God so loved the world that he gave his one and only Son, that whoever believes in him shall not perish but have eternal life." Verse 17 continues, "For God did not send his Son into the world to condemn the world, but to save the world through him." God saw the human dilemma—your dilemma—and sought to intervene. You need to respond by placing your trust in what He did for you.

Humans place their trust in a lot of different things only to be let down in the end. People disappoint. Aspirations disappoint. We disappoint ourselves. We become used to unfulfilled promises and become resolved to go on accepting the fact life will be an ongoing frustrating journey. Jesus came to earth to change all that, but we must realize that we are a large part of our own problem. Humans must ultimately come to the end of themselves and trust in Christ to experience real change.

No one will receive eternal life as a result of his or her own merit. People must accept the truth that they don't have ability to earn God's favor. All their goodness is not good enough.

God's standards of righteousness are far purer than ours. He does not grade on a bell-shaped curve. People need a different kind of righteousness, the kind Jesus alone can deliver.

The good news is that He has delivered this righteousness and we can receive it by faith. Jesus offers complete forgiveness from our sins, perfect righteousness through His death, and the promise of eternal life. But we must let go of our own feeble attempts at pleasing God and humbly receive the free gift.

Surrender

Finally, God requires that we surrender our lives completely to Him. We must accept that our lives are not our own, but belong to Him. Since God gave us life in the first place, surrender is a reasonable response. It is possible only when we recognize that He created us for a purpose and, as a result, He has the prerogative over our lives. It must also be remembered that God holds our lives in His hands and we continue to exist because He breathes life into us.

Surrender implies repenting of our old self-centered way of life. The word *repentance* means to turn around and have a change of mind and heart. It is a 180-degree turn and not a 90-degree one.

When we think of surrender we often have the image of a person with hands in the air submitting to the control of another. That is exactly what it means in this context. The person fully submits their life to the control of Christ, making Him Lord over every aspect. We can do this because we trust that the God who assumes control is good and will bring about something in the end that is infinitely superior to what we now have.

Acknowledgments

The art of story was unchartered territory for me at least in written form. Because it was an entirely unique undertaking, I enlisted individuals to help me in this endeavor. Comments and suggestions given to me were an enormous assistance as I sought to tell my personal story.

I would like to thank the following people:

- LaDonna Freisen who reviewed my manuscript and made invaluable suggestions to enhance its readability;
- Ken Peckett who gave me important guidance as I neared the conclusion of the project and guided me through numerous challenges;
- Donna Swinford who ably aided me through the editing process;
- and Sarah Simmons who provided layout assistance.

In addition, I owe an incredible debt to so many wonderful people who have been influential to me over the years. A number of these individuals have been described throughout my story, so I will refrain from mentioning them here. I would however like to express deep appreciation to members and friends from Trinity Assembly of God, Cazenovia Assembly of God, members of my Sunday School class at Life 360 Park Crest, the incarcerated men residing at the United States Medical Center for Federal Prisoners, the many students and faculty of Central Bible College and Evangel University, as well as colleagues in ministry whose lives have shaped the work of God in my life over many years.

I would like to also thank my wonderful family. Specifically, I owe a debt to my sister Alice who has shared much of this journey with me. I want to also thank my wonderful in-laws who in a very real sense shaped the meaning of family in my thinking: Barbara's mother Olga and father George, George's current wife Kay, Barbara's sisters, Patty and Karen, their husbands, Stephen and Ed, and brother Bob. Barb's family provided visual pictures of family life that were extremely formational.

When it comes to life formation however, few individuals possess greater potential to shape a person than one's children and grandchildren. My sons, Josh, Ben, and Nate, have been and will always be the most special of gifts. As they grew into men, they transitioned from sons to raise into my best friends. My grandchildren, Harrison, Adelynn, Samuel, Titus, and Lily, along with my daughters-in-law Brooke and Rachael have been cherished additions to our family.

Finally, my wife Barb has always been God's greatest gift to me. She is my closest confidant, my cherished life companion, and my unceasing source of joy. In every moment of happiness and sorrow of my adult life, she has been my constant support whose mere presence has been so sustaining.

CHILDHOOD HOME VIEWED TODAY

SONS OF JACOB SYNAGOGUE

MOM, UNCLE ELI, GRANDMA AND GRANDPOP SALTER,
DAD
ME, ALICE

BAR MITZVAH

BARBARA AND I TODAY

Jesus Storybook Bible